FINDING A NANNY FOR YOUR CHILD IN THE SAN FRANCISCO BAY AREA

A Step-by-Step Workbook with Local Resources in Eight Bay Area Counties

by

Alyce Desrosiers, LCSW

David W. Greenthal, Esq., Editor

Pince-Nez Press

San Francisco

Finding a Nanny For Your Child in the San Francisco Bay
Area

ISBN 1-930074-00-X
Library of Congress Catalog Card No. 00-132915

Cover design, page design & layout: Idintdoit Design
Fonts: Janson Text, Andale Mono, Futura, Comic Sans MS
Printing: Publishers Press

Pince-Nez Press
San Francisco, CA 94107
(415) 267-5978 *fax (800) 579-3614*
www.pince-nez.com
info@pince-nez.com

ACKNOWLEDGMENTS

This book would not have been possible without the never-ending support, great sense of humor, and unfailing clear vision of Michael Katz. He has been truly inspirational.

Thanks also to Susan Vogel who believed in the need for this book and never turned back. Also, thanks to David Greenthal who spent hours fleshing out the rough ideas in the book and massaging them into clear pictures.

I am deeply grateful to Kadija Johnson for her remarkable insight into the complexities of the relationship parents create with their caregivers and children. Her insight and direction formed the basis for the ideas in this book.

None of this could have been possible without my parents. My deepest thanks to them for teaching me the values of hard work, cooperation, empathy, and loyalty. Also to my five brothers, three sisters, five sisters-in-law, three brothers-in-law, and many nieces and nephews who showed me how to love and recognize their individual differences and the joys of depending on each other.

Deepest thanks to the parents who invited me into their lives and into their process of choosing nannies for their children. Without them this book could not have been written.

Thanks also to the many wonderful, competent, and loving nannies I have met and worked with over the years. Their enduring love and commitment to the children and families they work with is a constant source of inspiration. Many others have contributed significantly to the book: Laurel Kloonek, Robert Scott, and Kenny Altman at Parents' Place; Eunice Morales at the Perinatal Education and Lactation Center, CPMC; and Marsha Podd at the Center for Creative Parenting, for their continuing support of workshops for parents; Margaret Felton, President, and Cindy Schatt, Co-President of the Bay Area Nanny Association and Deborah Davis, Ph.D., editor of the National Nanny Newsletter, who have supported nannies and families in learning how to work together; Lynn Peterson, Director of PFC Information Services, and MaryBeth Philips, Director and Founder of TrustLine, who have supported parents for years by checking into the criminal histories of nanny applicants and have spent hours educating parents, policymakers, and nannies about the vitally important need to conduct background checks.

Many other friends and colleagues must be mentioned: David and Marilee Skolnik, for their marketing and editing ideas and support; Laurie Frankel, for graphic design; and Judy Turiel, for editing and writing; my friends and fellow-flight attendants at Delta Air Lines, who encouraged me to follow my dreams; Professor-Emeritus Art Emlen, Portland State University, who helped make them happen; and Jeree Pawl, Ph.D., former Director of the Infant Parent Program, UCSF, who first introduced me to child care issues and the development of relationships between parents and children.

Finally, to the hundreds of nannies, parents, and their children, to the parenting agencies, mother's groups, nanny placement agencies, child care educators and researchers, child therapists and developmental specialists, who unselfishly gave me insight into the complexities of the work they do, my deepest gratitude. I hope I have presented your experiences in the way you would want me to.

DEDICATION

This book is dedicated to Michael Katz for his never-ending love, support, guidance, and direction. Without him, this book could not have been written.

CONTENTS

CHAPTER III: THE ESSENTIALS

CHAPTER IV: THE SEARCH

CHAPTER V: THE SELECTION PROCESS

CHAPTER VI: LEGAL ISSUES

LEGAL STUFF

This book provides parents with extensive resources to assist them in their nanny search. Not all resources listed are personally known to the author and neither the author nor the publisher makes any guarantee as to the competency of the agencies, public health clinics, CPR/First Aid providers, or any other resources listed herein. Furthermore, laws change regularly and specific counties and cities may have their own laws and ordinances pertaining to the topics addressed in this book. Parents are therefore advised to consult their own attorneys prior to hiring and contracting with a caregiver.

introduction

HOW TO USE THIS BOOK

Mary stood in front of the bulletin board unable to move. In the infant carrier strapped to her belly slept three-month-old Tommy. Mary looked down at Tommy and then up at the bulletin board, literally paralyzed by the pieces of paper swimming in front of her. Here were over 125 handwritten notes written by people she didn't know. "Caregivers Seeking Employment, F/T, P/T, Either, Share Care, Parents Seeking Caregiver." Mary stared and read, "I love babies," "Mother of three will love yours," "I am student from Brazil. I can work days," "No Hablo English," "I have good reference." Mary panicked. Her eyes blurred. "Where do I start?"

Mary is not alone. She stands among many other parents in her child care crisis. Approximately sixty-two percent of mothers in the workforce have children under the age of three. (U.S. Dept. of Labor, 1999) Fifty-seven percent have a child under one year. All parents need to find a child care solution that works. In the state of California, 51% of children younger than five with parents in the workforce are in child care outside the family. (California Child Care Resource & Referral Network, 1997) Among the remaining 49%, many work out a solution by using family or relatives. An unknown number of parents look for someone to come into their home to take care of their child—someone we call a "nanny," an "au-pair," or a "caregiver." (Demographics on in-home child care are scarce and difficult to find, primarily because the market is unlicensed and unregulated.)

If you are a parent of an infant you may not have a choice but to look for a nanny. In San Francisco and the Bay Area only three to seven percent of all slots in child care centers are for children from zero to two years old. (Child Care Resource and Referral Network)

If you are a parent working an unusual or changing schedule, you also may not have a choice. In California, only 2% of child care centers and 29% of family day care centers open their doors before 6:30 a.m. and stay open after 6:00 p.m. (Child Care Resource and Referral Network,)

If you are a busy, overwhelmed stay-at-home parent who needs an extra hand with your kids, you may not have a choice. Dropping off and picking up your child at a day care center may make your life more complicated than bringing someone to your own home to help out.

You may be a parent who makes the choice to hire a nanny because you want your child to stay home and get individual attention from one person, surrounded by what is familiar.

Regardless of your reason for choosing to hire a nanny, you may find yourself, like many parents, feeling quite overwhelmed by the process. You may find yourself standing paralyzed in front of bulletin boards just as Mary did. You may find yourself frantically calling friends, neighbors, and colleagues. With a knot in your stomach you may place a domestic help wanted ad in the *San Francisco Chronicle*. You may act instinctively without really having a plan or strategy. Your usual good judgment about how to make important decisions may be seriously compromised.

There is a good reason for this. What is expected of parents IS paralyzing!

Parents are expected to ask a complete stranger to come into their home and take care of the most important person in their lives. They leave this stranger alone with their child, unsupervised, and unobserved.

You may be worried, asking "How will I know what person I can trust? How will I know who will be a good fit for me and my child? How will I know what I need to know in order to choose?"

All parents, regardless of their child care situation, ask these questions. It would be worrisome if they didn't. Yet the "worry factor" is raised considerably higher for parents hiring a nanny. The reason:

This is an unlicensed and unregulated market.

Literally anyone can say he or she wants to take care of children. Parents hiring nannies come across a wide range of qualified and unqualified applicants. Some are people with many years' experience raising their own children and others. Many nanny applicants are students of early childhood education. You may encounter teachers from Mexico, doctors from Russia, and nurses from the Philippines, some of whom may not have documentation to work legally in the U.S. You also may hear from applicants who may be unemployable in any other job because of a range of factors: lack of education, language barriers, or personal histories characterized by drug abuse or financial or legal problems. (In this book, child care providers are assumed to be women since the overwhelming majority who apply for this position are women. Parents are usually referred to in the plural, not out of insensitivity to single parents, but to simplify the use of pronouns.)

This eclectic array of applicants is one of the things that makes the choice of a nanny so difficult. There are many decisions you need to make beyond knowing who would fit with you and your child. You need answers to essential questions before even starting: Should I hire someone who does not possess the necessary documents to work legally in the U.S.? If so, what are my risks with the Internal Revenue Service and the Immigration and Naturalization Service? How much English is important for her to know? How does legal status and her ability to speak English affect what I pay and the quality of care I get?

There are other questions. Where do I find a nanny? How do I check references? What questions should I ask during an interview and what answers should I listen for? Should I put together a contract? Is it important to do a criminal background check? Are CPR and First Aid courses necessary? Is a TB test necessary?

Getting the answers to these questions takes time and energy but it's not enough:

Finding and choosing a nanny is both an emotional and a pragmatic process.

How you feel about leaving your child alone with someone who is at first only a stranger can affect your usual good judgment. The process of choosing can be an emotional roller coaster ride. You may feel a range of emotions throughout the process: excitement, disappointment, uncertainty, fear, relief, and resolution. These feelings can come unannounced and strike with intensity. They can also make it very difficult for you to make a good, timely decision.

This book will guide you through the pragmatic process of finding a nanny. It also will help you recognize the range of emotions you may experience. (♥ Heart icons signal a discussion of the emotions parents may experience through the process.) This book will prepare you to make an informed and meaningful choice. The questions posed in the following chapters may seem insurmountable at first. They're not. If you take the approach the book provides, you will increase your odds of choosing wisely so that everyone gets off to a good start. As such, it's best to read this book all the way through *before* beginning the process.

i.
Is a nanny right for my family?

ILLUSION VS. REALITY

There's been a lot in the news lately about nannies and au pairs and the parents who choose them. Most of the news isn't good news. Nannies are often thought of as falling at either end of a spectrum ranging from Angels of Mercy to Murderesses from Hell. The parents who choose them are often thought of as either self-centered and irresponsible (when they choose the Murderess) or lucky and privileged (when they choose the Angel of Mercy).

The reality, of course, is that parents and caregivers are not so easily characterized, and the process they experience in choosing each other is at best both complex and difficult.

Every parent wants the best care for his or her child. Most have a vision about who their "ideal" caregiver would be. Often this vision is a collection of ideal characteristics taken from real life experiences. The collection can include positive attributes such as being wise, nurturing, loving, reliable, and always present when needed. The collection can also include the absence of negative characteristics such as being unreliable, inattentive, or emotionally indifferent.

This ideal image is, however, an illusion. Caregivers are human, after all, and we expect a great deal from them, namely to take on the complex responsibility of caring for someone else's child, to get close enough to nurture a child and yet maintain enough distance so as not to threaten mom's or dad's closeness, and to nurture a child for years and then leave because the child doesn't need a nanny anymore. The responsibilities and emotional capabilities required of a nanny demand a very special type of person.

Every parent wants to find someone sooner rather than later. Every parent wants the process to be uncomplicated with a responsible, reliable, and loving nanny just a few phone calls away. In short, most parents want an Angel of Mercy to walk into their home immediately and make everything right.

This ideal process of choosing a caregiver is, however, also an illusion. More often, the search involves four to six weeks of placing ads, talking to everyone you know, prescreening forty to fifty applicants, checking references, interviewing, and then contracting. The whole process can require twenty to forty hours of hard work.

♥ The process is also a roller-coaster trip with you and your emotions hanging on for the wild ride. You find someone you like and trust, but then she doesn't show up and doesn't answer your frantic calls to find out why. You interview someone who says all the right things and then she meets your child and responds to him like the Murderess from Hell. You're constantly weighing the odds. She'll be loyal, but then over-protect your child. She'll stimulate his development, but then leave to develop her career. She knows a lot about kids, but she'll take over and be "the Mom." ❤

In the meantime, the clock is ticking. You wake up at 3:00 a.m. in a panic. You need to hire someone by next week. Should you be so picky? You sit by the phone and wait for a caregiver to return your calls. Has someone given her a better offer? Once you are certain about knowing who would be right, you nevertheless question your judgment. You feel guilty every day for burdening the relatives or friends who are helping you out until you can find a nanny.

Rest assured you *can* find the right nanny. Many wonderful nannies are nurturing young children and helping their parents along the way. Many become part of the family and stay for years. Knowing what to expect before you start and keeping your emotions steady during the process will get you there.

CHILD CARE OPTIONS

I feel I had no choice but to hire a nanny. As a single mother with newborn, premature twins, I needed around-the-clock care.—
Mother of two-week-old twins

My son's family day care closed its doors after four years. I found another family day care, but he didn't fit in. He was older, the curriculum was too structured, the teachers couldn't give him the individual attention he needed. Hiring a nanny was the best decision we made. It's like having a big brother for my son.—
Parents who hired a male nanny for their son

I wanted to hire a nanny. Schlepping my kids to someone else's house every morning and then back at night was just more chaos than I could handle! I started interviewing, and it was a nightmare. The clock kept ticking, and I had to hire someone. My friend told me about this family day care across town. I drove over. The woman who ran the day care was exactly who I wanted. The situation wasn't. I opted for the person and now I schlepp—but I feel I made the right choice. My kids are doing very well there!— Working parent of two children under age two

There are a lot of practical advantages to hiring a nanny. Your child gets to stay at home surrounded by familiar sights, sounds, and smells. Your child goes through daily routines with one person who gets to know him well. You avoid having to prepare your little one to leave the house in the morning, drive across town in traffic, and do the drop off and the pick up later that day. If you're running late after work, you don't have to worry that the day care center will send your child to the police department (this happens!) or that you'll have to take out a loan to pay the late pick-up fines. If your child is sick, you don't lose a day's pay or have to take a sick day.

Now, if all that sounds like hiring a nanny is the way to go, hold on. It's expensive. The average hourly cost for a nanny in San Francisco and the Bay Area is $12- $15 per hour with a trend to $18-$20! The $25,000 to $31,000 annual cost for forty hours a week of care can be prohibitive for a family. The expense can make a parent wonder whether it's worthwhile to work. By comparison, family day care or child care centers range in cost from $10,200 to $14,000 per year.

❤ The other challenge is the worry factor. Your nanny is alone at home unsupervised with your child. You have to learn to trust her. ❤

Finally, you are an employer to your nanny. This role includes handling the paperwork to pay taxes and securing the liability insurance to protect yourself. Additionally, keep in mind that a nanny's presence in your home will reduce your family's privacy.

But then, you may not have a real choice. Many parents simply cannot find an available slot at either a family day care or a child care center. They choose to hire a nanny because they have no other choices.

DEFINITIONS

Nanny. According to the International Nanny Association (INA), a nanny is someone who comes into a parent's home and provides individual loving, responsible, and nurturing child care. The actual responsibilities are unique to each parent-nanny relationship but most often include full care for the child, including any housekeeping related to his or her care, and running errands.

Au-Pair. An au-pair is a European woman between the ages of 18 and 25 years who comes to the U.S. under the auspices of a program managed by the U.S. Information Agency (USIA). Au-pairs are under contract for one year to provide a maximum of 45 hours per week of child care for children over three months of age in exchange for the cultural experience of living in the U.S. and a small salary (approximately $1,600 per month including room and board). Parents pay an agency fee (approximately $3,500), transportation to bring the au-pair to the U.S., and a return ticket home at the end of the year (or sooner if she doesn't work out!).

Many parents are very hesitant to hire au-pairs after the 1998 Louise Woodward murder trial which showed how difficult it can be for a young woman to take full responsibility for young children for long hours at a time while living in an unfamiliar country without the social and emotional support of close family and friends.

Governess. A governess is a woman whose primary responsibility is to educate a child on the academic and social skills necessary to navigate the world. She also provides custodial care for the child only.

Mother's Helper. A mother's helper is a woman who helps a stay-at-home mom with as-needed child care, light housekeeping, and errands.

Baby Nurses and Doulas. There are two types of doulas, a birth doula and a post-partum doula.

A birth doula provides the following services:

1. Physical, emotional, and informational support to mothers and their partners during labor and birth;
2. Help and advice on comfort measures such as breathing, relaxation, massage, and positioning;
3. Assistance to families in gathering information about the course of labor and the options regarding labor;
4. Continuous emotional reassurance and comfort;
5. Non-medical assistance such as massage and other non-pharmacological pain relief measures;
6. Assistance to partners who want to play an active support role;

7. Help so the mother has a safe and satisfying childbirth as the mother defines it.

What does it take to be a doula?

Almost anyone with a desire to help birthing women and their families can be a doula. Some doulas are trained and certified, others just have on-the-job experience. For more information on doulas and where to find doulas see page 185 of the Resources chapter.

Post-partum doulas are woman who are trained or experienced in providing postpartum care to both mother and baby. Their responsibilities include:

1. Breast-feeding support and advice;
2. Cooking;
3. Child care;
4. Errands; and
5. Light cleaning for the family.

What makes a doula different from a full-time nanny?

1. Cost: Doulas charge $15-$28 per hour. Many require a $1,000 retainer. Average nanny fees (live out) are $12-$15 per hour with an upward trend toward $18-$20.
2. Availability: Doulas should be booked several months in advance. Most nannies are available within 2-4 weeks of hiring.
3. Scheduling: Doulas often work nights/weekends and around-the-clock. Nannies may have the flexibility in their lives to be available during these hours, but such scheduling must be negotiated.

4. Education and training: Doulas who have attended training participate in two-day conferences covering:
   - Breast feeding;
   - Baby nourishment;
   - Postpartum depression;
   - First Aid and infant CPR training;
   - Post C-section care; and
   - What to look for in newborn illness.
5. Experience: Many doulas do not attend a course but have experience with infants. Many nannies do not attend courses but have experience with infants.
6. Special needs: Many doulas have experience with special needs infants, such as multiples or premature babies, or with medically-fragile infants. Nannies may have similar experience.

There's an increasing trend among parents, particularly parents of multiples or medically-fragile babies or parents without family support, to hire a baby nurse or doula postpartum. Baby nurses and doulas differ in their levels of education and training but not in the services they provide. The quality of the service depends on the individual's experience with the specific needs of the particular children and parenting philosophies of the individual parents.

Child Care Centers. Child care centers can be referred to as day care, nursery schools, preschools, or center-based programs. Center philosophies vary, but their goals usually focus on meeting a child's physical, cognitive, and developmental needs. Social and self-help skills are usually emphasized and programs are often designed to promote school readiness. Centers are generally licensed to operate in facilities (commercial buildings, churches, private schools), rather than homes, and the centers can be private or public. Families who meet low income guidelines are sometimes eligible for subsidized child care programs, which may be free or charge fees on a sliding scale. Subsidized centers tend to have long waiting lists, so it is best to apply as early in advance as possible. Some private centers may have scholarships for low income parents. Most centers require that children be toilet-trained, but a few centers accept infants and toddlers. Specialized infant/toddler centers tend to be very expensive and may have long waiting lists. Centers often have fixed hours of availability, commonly 7:00 a.m. to 6:00 p.m. Some centers will care for children on odd schedules, weekends, or on a drop-in basis. Average costs in San Francisco for these centers are approximately $1,159 a month for infants through age two and $850 per month for ages two through five. (2000 figures)

Family Child Care Homes. These are programs operated in the caregiver's own home. In California, these programs must be licensed. Family child care homes are sometimes flexible regarding fees, hours, drop-in care, accepting a sick child, and caring for a child over the weekend. Family child care tends to be one of the least expensive child care options. Average full-time monthly fees for infant care at family day care homes in San Francisco are $850 for infants to age two and $800 for ages two to five.

In California, family day care centers account for only 31% of all child care slots, so many parents find it difficult to find an opening in a family day care center. If you are interested in this type of care for your child, it is wise to contact your local Child Care Information Resource and Referral agency ("IR&R") early to see what slots are available in your neighborhood. Parents often put their child's name on a waiting list months ahead of time. (See pages 177-184 of the Resources chapter for IR&Rs in your area.)

Family child care homes are licensed for children from birth to 12 years of age, but some prefer to care for only specific age groups (*i.e.*, toddlers or school age). Typically, family child care homes are licensed for six children, including the provider's own children, with no more than three children under the age of two. Some are licensed for 12 to 14 children depending on their ages; these expanded programs must have a full-time assistant.

The quality of care in family day care and child care centers is determined in part by turnover rates. A lower turnover rate will translate to greater consistency in care and a greater likelihood your child will be taken care of by people who come to know him well. Consult with your local IR&R for additional information on quality of care or contact www.childrenscouncil.org. For preschools in San Francisco (including preschools that provide infant care), see *Finding a Preschool For Your Child in San Francisco*, by Lori Rifkin, Ph.D., Vera Obermeyer, Ph.D., and Irene Byrne, listed on page 199.

License Exempt Providers. Child care providers who care in their own homes for the children of only one family other than their own are exempt from licensing in California. If providers care for more than one family, the facility is required to be licensed by the state as a family day care home.

PROS AND CONS OF IN-HOME CHILD CARE

PROS

- Flexibility in the hours and days that care is provided
- Consistency in child's normal daily routines
- Individual attention for the child
- No transportation necessary to and from child care center
- In-home sick child care
- Control over who is hired to care for your child
- Selection from a larger pool of caregivers for infant care than family day care or day care centers
- Cost-effective if more than one child is being cared for
- Light housekeeping, such as errands, laundry, etc., can be negotiated.

CONS

- Reduced privacy and reduced living space
- Lack of supervision when the parent is out of the home
- Need to negotiate the complexities of being an employer to someone you invite into your family life and home
- Demands of being an employer, such as paying payroll taxes, etc.
- More expensive than family day care or day care centers. In San Francisco/Bay Area the average costs are $12-$15 per hour with a trend upwards to $18-$20 per hour. Annual costs for a 40-hour week can range from $25,000-$31,000.
- Unlicensed and unregulated market, requiring thorough checking of background and credentials of each applicant.

WORKSHEET

Pros of having a nanny in our home:

_____

_____

_____

_____

_____

Cons:

_____

_____

_____

_____

_____

ii.
getting started

GETTING STARTED

I don't have a clue .... —first-time parent

I found our first nanny by luck. She was an angel who stayed with our family for two years. Since then we've had five nannies from hell! I don't trust my judgment anymore. —second-time parent

I need a road map.—(almost every parent)

This chapter provides a roadmap—an overview of how to proceed in finding a nanny. It outlines the various pieces you will use during the process. In the following sections, we will look more closely at what goes into each piece and how to put these pieces together so they will work for you.

But first you should be aware of the emotional aspects of embarking on this journey.

♥ **Uncertainty.** Many parents feel "clueless" about what they need to know to choose a nanny. This is particularly true if you are a first-time parent. After all, you may feel less than certain yourself about being "qualified" for the job of parenting! You may find yourself saying, "I don't even know what questions I should be asking during an interview. What feels worse is that I'm not even sure what answers to listen for! Someone could be saying all the right things, like 'I love kids,' but is that enough? I know I want someone trustworthy and nurturing, but how can I tell if someone is nurturing and loving just by talking with her?"

At the other end of the uncertainty spectrum are those parents who have done it too many times before. They've had more than their fair share of Nannies from Hell! Perhaps they chose a woman who watched the soaps all day and ignored the kids. Or a teenager who was more interested in having her friends over than caring for the baby. Or a caregiver who never told them she was court-ordered into drug treatment.

These experiences can make parents begin to question their judgment. Going through a second, third, or fourth round of searching most certainly must mean they "failed" at the first, second, and third round. This time they are determined to find the ideal caregiver, even though they know an ideal caregiver doesn't exist. They're stuck. Their uncertainty about their ability to choose may put them in a position of not being able to choose at all.

♥ **Separation.** Separations are an integral and inevitable part of life. Our first introductions to them begin in the very early years of our lives. Hiring a nanny and leaving your child alone with her is one of those important beginnings for your child.

Saying good-bye to your child can be as hard for you as it is for your child. Many parents worry "Will she be safe?" "Am I neglecting my responsibility as a parent?" "Will she be mad at me for leaving?" and "Will she remember who I am when I come back?" Most parents feel torn when faced with a crying child begging them to stay or an ambivalent child ignoring them when they return.

Your child will have different reactions to separations as she goes through the expectable stages of development. Your child's temperament will also affect how she reacts to separations. Your own needs and beliefs about separations add to the mix. All affect your ability to choose a nanny and to work with your nanny when the inevitable separations occur.

This a very brief introduction to an important topic you may want to consider further. You may find it helpful to refer to the following for a more thorough discussion: "The Dance of Separation," *Becoming the Parent You Want To Be*, Laura Davis and Janet Keyser (New York: Broadway Books, 1997); *The Emotional Life of the Toddler*, Alicia Lieberman, Ph.D. (New York: The Free Press, 1998); www.zerotothree.org.

♥ **Guilt, longing and anxiety.** Most parents feel responsible for making sure their child is safe and nurtured. Some parents, however, feel unusually responsible and anxious. If you add to this a good amount of longing to be with the child, you get a very complicated and difficult mixture. This mix of guilt, longing, and anxiety can make it very difficult for a parent to leave the baby with *anyone*, no matter how much experience the person has. If the baby cries more than five minutes, then certainly it's the parent who is responsible for soothing the baby. If the toddler screams and cries when the parents leave in the morning for work, then certainly they should stay home and take care of the child. Most parents eventually realize they can't be completely responsible for their child's well-being, nor can they be in two places at once! But the guilt, longing, and anxiety they feel can make it very difficult to get started choosing someone who can take some responsibility for their child and do it well.

♥ **Envy and jealousy.** The green-eyed monster in the closet can be alive and well for many parents choosing a nanny. Just the thought of someone else spending time alone laughing, cooing, and playing with their child can set the twinges of jealousy on fire! Beneath these twinges lies the worry that someone else gets the first prize. Perhaps the caregiver will become Mom. No amount of reassurance that Mom is always Mom to a child helps. The worry about being replaced is there. The envy and jealousy are there.

The most important point about these feelings is that they're normal and expectable. They are unique to each person depending on his or her own histories and relationships growing up. They can be quite intense at times. They can get in your way of using your own good judgment about choosing a nanny. They can get in your way of even getting started.

It's important to recognize these emotions. They'll be there at various times and intensities throughout the process of choosing a nanny to care for your child.

While these emotions can complicate the process, if they are understood and managed, they can clarify your priorities and perspective on selecting a nanny.

NANNY-SEARCH CHECKLIST

The following checklist is a "road map" providing direction to find the right caregiver for your child.

1. Evaluate need:
   - A. The ideal caregiver
   - B. Parenting values and behaviors
   - C. Child's development and idiosyncrasies

2. Come up with a job description:
   - A. Child care duties and responsibilities
   - B. Household responsibilities
   - C. Hours of work
   - D. Salary and benefits

3. Announce the job:
   - A. Post on bulletin boards
   - B. Newspapers
   - C. Contact friends, colleagues, family
   - D. Web Sites

3. Draft a job application:
   - A. Name, address, and telephone number
   - B. Marital status
   - C. Number and ages of own children
   - D. Personality and character
   - E. Previous child care experience: who, when, what and for how long
   - F. Reasons for leaving

G. Work traits, e.g., responsibility, reliability, initiative, communication, etc.

H. Understanding of child development and a child's personal idiosyncrasies

I. Experience in negotiating stages of development with different children

J. "Fit" with my child's personality and idiosyncrasies

K. "Fit" with our parenting values and behaviors

L. Salary requirements

M. Legal status

N. California driver's license and own car

O. CPR, First Aid, TB, Hepatitis

4. Prescreening the applicants

A. Previous work experience

B. Salary expectations

C. CPR, First Aid, TB, background check

D. References: names and telephone numbers of three references

5. Get references:

A. Verify dates, responsibilities, reasons for leaving

B. Discuss personality, knowledge, work traits, communication style, etc.

C. Evaluate risks and harm: substance abuse, child abuse or neglect, etc.

6. Begin the interview process
    A. First interview
           1. Evaluation of work experience,
               personality and character, "fit" with my child
           2. Follow-up interview scheduled

    B. Second interview
           1. Clarification and continuation of above
           2. Meets with my child
           3. "Fit" with my child

    C. Third interview
           Clarification and continuation of above

7. Order a background check:
    Criminal record checked with TrustLine Registry
    and/or PFC Information Services

8. Agree on a contract/working agreement:
    A. Terms written and clarified
    B. Translated if needed
    C. Signed

EVALUATION OF NEED

How you are is as important as what you do. —Jeree Pawl, Ph.D., Former Director, Infant Parent Program, University of California, San Francisco

If you want to be successful in finding a nanny, you need to know what you want before starting: that means *who* you want, *what* you want her to do, and *how* you want her to be with your child. In this chapter we take a close look at the *who* and *how* part of that need. In the next chapter we'll look at the *what* part of that need.

Some parents consider who they want only in terms of a nanny's job responsibilities, *i.e.*, what she is going to do. They need someone to care for their child certain hours and days and to take the responsibility to ensure that their child is safe and nurtured.

They stop here. They believe that expecting anything more from a caregiver is gravy. They feel relieved just knowing someone shows up on time and stays until they come home and that their child is not harmed.

After reading this book, you won't stop there. Nannies who just "watch" kids don't exist. Nannies have relationships with kids they care for and with their parents. This is the most fundamental reason why it's important to consider *who* a nanny is and *how* she cares for children. This is also why it's important to consider who you are as a parent and who your child is. Each of these parties—the nanny, child, and parents—enters into a relationship that determines what the nanny does with the child and how she does it.

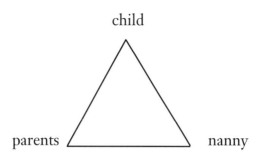

child

parents   nanny

Once this evaluation is complete, you will have plenty of questions to ask prospective applicants during an interview, and you will know what sort of responses to listen for to determine whether this is someone you can trust and someone who would be a good fit for you and your child. Now that's a lot to get out of one chapter!

Research over the years on infant and toddler development has shown us that human relationships are the foundations on which children build their futures. (*Zero to Three*: National Center for Infants, Toddlers and Families) The relationships that children make in their very early years shape their expectations of themselves and others. The quality of these relationships affect their sense of themselves as lovable, competent, and desirable people. Early experiences affect the kind of relationships they create in their adult lives. All meaningful relationships count—those among a child, her parents, and every member of her family, those between a child and her caregiver, and also those between the family and caregiver.

That's why it's so important that you wonder about the *who* and the *how*. Who your nanny is and how she relates to your child define the quality of the relationship between the nanny and your child. The relationship your child develops with a nanny has meaning that develops over time through their daily interactions. The meaning develops through what each person does and also by how each is. How does a nanny soothe a crying baby? With gentle rocking and a quiet lullaby or by bouncing him up and down on a hard knee? How does a nanny discipline a toddler? Firmly and clearly with a calm voice or erratically in a loud, harsh, angry voice. How does a nanny meet your child for the first time? By picking him up right away and hugging him or standing to the side and saying hello with a warm, friendly voice?

In this chapter we look at:

• who a nanny might be
• who you are as parents
• who your child is.

Putting these elements together tells you a lot about what you need that is unique and specific to your family. Likewise, this chapter will help you distinguish between nannies you are interested in hiring and those you won't even consider. You can and will make an informed decision.

WHO WOULD BE THE IDEAL NANNY?

The ideal nanny for my child would be my mother. —parent

The ideal nanny for my child would certainly not be my mother. —parent

The ideal nanny would be me. —parent

You really have to click with the people you work for. I've worked for some people for two weeks and thought, 'I'm not gonna make it any longer. I just don't like these people.' It seems that everyone has to be on the same wavelength, especially as far as the child goes. We have to have the same ideas about what to do and how to do it. Of course there are differences, but at least you have to be able to talk about them. —caregiver

If the ideal nanny walked through your door today who would that person be?

If you were to consider all the people you have known in your life, who would you want to care for your child? Is it your own mother, your sister, best friend, or next door neighbor? What is it about this person that makes her seem ideal?

For some parents, who they would *not* want is clearer. For these parents, repairing or breaking a cycle of poor parenting or learning from past painful experiences may have more meaning. You may want to ask yourself what it is about this person that makes her seem less than ideal. What characteristics or personality traits does this person have, or not have, that make her seem less than the perfect nanny?

Just as parenting styles differ, so do nannies' styles of caregiving.

One family decided they would want the photographer who recently did a series of photos of their nine-month-old son. The woman was in her mid-20's, educated, artistic, creative, and full of energy. She had clear goals and aspirations about her life and had strong opinions about children, which she freely gave. For this family of professionals, education and expressing opinions freely is important. They enjoyed lively discussions and lots of different activities with their son.

Another family wanted someone like the mother's sister, who had two children in elementary school. For this family it was very important their four-month-old son learn to respect others and to know his manners when visiting a new place. They wanted someone like mom's sister, who could set limits firmly and consistently while letting their son have a good time running, jumping, and playing with others.

A single mother with premature twins wanted a "wife and a mother." She needed someone who had "been there before" raising twins, since she had not. She needed someone to share the around-the-clock feedings, someone who knew how to feed two infants at once, someone who knew how to calm a crying infant when the other was sleeping, someone who could manage the laundry, grocery shopping and the twins' routines. Someone who would stay for a long time.

Another family with a three-year-old mildly autistic son wanted someone they had never met but could only imagine—someone with experience caring for children with special needs. They needed to be certain the caregiver would know the importance of routines and talking with them daily about their son's behavior. They needed someone active and bright who could laugh easily when the going got rough. They also wanted someone who had "pulled herself up by her bootstraps" and knew first-hand how hard work can pay off.

Here is a sample of some character traits that parents often want in a caregiver. It may be helpful to use this list in evaluating what it is about your ideal caregiver that makes her seem ideal.

- Warm
- Caring
- Active
- Responsible
- Cheerful
- Open
- Honest
- Calm
- Shy
- Mature
- Bright
- Logical
- Emotional
- Pleases others

- Nurturing
- Loving
- Patient
- Reliable
- Takes initiative
- Direct
- Independent
- Quiet
- Exuberant
- Spirited
- Well-groomed
- Pragmatic
- Lively

Knowing the desired positive characteristics is not enough. There are certain characteristics most parents want to avoid in a caregiver.

- Harsh
- Critical
- Needing a lot of direction

- Punishing
- Controlling

45

WORKSHEET:

WHO IS MY IDEAL NANNY

1. If the ideal nanny were to walk in your door today, who would that person be?

_____

_____

2. What is it about this person that makes her seem ideal?

_____

_____

3. Characteristics of this person:

- Warm
- Nurturing
- Caring
- Loving
- Active
- Patient
- Responsible
- Reliable
- Cheerful
- Open
- Direct
- Spirited
- Honest
- Independent
- Calm
- Quiet
- Shy
- Exuberant
- Mature
- Well-groomed
- Bright
- Pragmatic
- Logical
- Lively

- Emotional
- Pleases Others
- Takes Initiative
- Others:_____

  _____

  _____

4. Characteristics we want to avoid:

  _____

  _____

  _____

5. Special considerations of a nanny. Do you need someone with special experience?
   - Experience with multiples or more than one child
   - Experience with children's medical conditions
   - Premature infants
   - Developmental delays
   - Asperger's syndrome
   - Autism
   - Rett's Disorder
   - Speech and language problems
   - Hearing impaired
   - Seeing impaired
   - Sleeping or feeding disturbances
   - Unusual difficulties in movement or coordination
   - Unusual behavior problems
   - Attention Deficit Disorder
   - Unusual difficulties separating from parents
   - Aggressive, out of control behavior

WHO AM I AS A PARENT?
PARENTING VALUES & BEHAVIOR

Describe the way your family likes to be together. How do you spend your days? What are the rhythms and routines of your daily lives?

No two families are alike. Each has a personality which characterizes it. Your family may be very active with a never-ending list of things to do and places to go. You may have an active social life, with friends and neighbors coming and going throughout the day or with endless social engagements. Routines may be made only to be broken when something else comes up. Family members may be expressive, laughing loudly or yelling to be heard. Other families are quieter, slower paced, predictably going through their daily routines and holding close to a few long-standing friends.

Families also go through changes brought about by the ages of the children and outside events not always in their control. The needs of an infant for nurturance and predictability in routines put different demands on parents and nannies than toddlers' needs for limits (as well as for somebody with the energy to run after them!). Some families grow more easily through one stage than another.

When considering your ideal nanny's qualities, it's helpful to know your family's unique characteristics in order to understand who would fit.

What are the three values you believe are most important for your child to learn about her world and how do you teach them?

A lot of parents are thrown off by this question. They feel it's a little heavy-handed to be talking about values when all one wants is to hire a nanny!

The reason the question is so very important is that how people—parents, nannies, and eventually children—behave depends in part on the values they hold.

Consider this dilemma that many parents face: It's 2 a.m. and you get the all-too-common wake-up call from your 14-month-old. The child is not hungry, wet, or hurt. One parent wants to pick up the baby while the other wants to let the baby "cry it out." The parent who wants to pick up the baby focuses on the value of dependence: The child needs to learn that "we will be there whenever he needs us." The other parent focuses on the value of independence, namely, the child needs to learn that "we can't be there for him all the time."

Nannies, just like parents, make decisions like this throughout the day. They respond to a child, just as parents do, based on their values. That's why it's so important to know your and your prospective nanny's values.

There are other values hidden beneath other ways parents respond to children. Imagine you have told your two-and-one-half-year-old daughter it's time to put away her toys and get ready for bed. She ignores you and continues to play. In response to the third attempt, she turns to you and says, "I hate you! Leave me alone! Go away!" One parent may respond by saying, "You can't talk to your mother that way. Now put away your toys. It's time for bed." Another parent may respond differently by saying, "I know you're mad at me, but it's time for bed. Now put away your toys, and let's get you ready for bed." One parent holds dearly to the value of respecting your elders. The other holds dearly to the value of respecting children's feelings, ideas, and opinions. They both hold to the value that children need to know they can't be the rulers of the house.

Your nanny has her own values. During the routines of daily life, she'll respond to your child in ways that reflect her values. It's important to recognize yours and learn about hers so you can see where the similarities and differences lie.

CULTURAL VALUES, HABITS, & CUSTOMS

We all learn from our families as well as from the culture we grew up in what is important about our world. These values shape our perceptions and influence what we feel is important for children to learn about their world. There can be an infinite variety of personal values within a particular culture.

In San Francisco and the Bay Area, parents have an opportunity to expose their children to the beauty of many different cultures.

During your search you likely will meet nannies from many different cultures. The values they learned growing up may be very different from yours. These values influence the way they respond to children just as yours do. Cultural differences can enrich our lives, create conflicts and misunderstandings, or both. If parents see a nanny behave in a way the parents don't quite understand, it is wise to first consider possible cultural differences before jumping to judgment.

One mother was shocked to come home and find her child's stomach covered in a fragrant essential oil. The nanny explained that in her culture crying babies are soothed by massaging them with this oil. The mother took a deep breath and asked more questions. Eventually she adopted the custom herself.

Some nannies, particularly from Latino and Filipino cultures, can be quite surprised at some family customs in the U.S. For example, it can be a foreign idea to them that babies would sleep in their own beds or even in a room separate from their parents. Similarly, letting a baby cry for 10 or 20 minutes until he learns to sleep on his own may "run against the grain" of what they see as "normal." Generally in traditional Latino and Filipino families babies are picked up right away when they cry and are often carried until the age of three. North American, Latino, and Filipino values, of course, are not misguided or misplaced. They evolved for complex reasons.

Similarly, in some cultures, respecting authority supersedes the value of respecting children's feelings or opinions. Children are routinely told to respect their elders. It simply may not be acceptable for children to tell older people or people in authority how they feel about them. Likewise, before visiting someone's home, children may be told how to behave so they learn to respect others' rules.

Knowing your own values, habits, and preferences and those of your nanny helps build a good relationship. You may want to explore with your nanny what values she feels are important for children to learn about their world and talk with her about how these values influence how she cares for children.

WORKSHEET:

WHAT ARE OUR VALUES?

How do the daily rhythms and routines of your family life reflect your parental values?

What is the one important piece of advice that was handed down to you by your parents that reflects a value you believe is important to teach a child?

What are the three most important values you believe are important for your child to learn about his world?

How do you teach these to your child in your daily interactions with him?

Which cultural values are consistent with and which are in conflict with what you want for your child?

Interview questions regarding values and culture:

_____

_____

_____

_____

_____

_____

_____

WHO IS MY CHILD IN TERMS OF DEVELOPMENT AND IDIOSYNCRASIES?

As all parents realize, every child has his or her own personality. Some babies come into the world screaming loud and clear while others barely give a whimper. Some babies, when put in their crib for a nap will be at the other end of the crib within ten minutes, while others are in the same spot where you left them. Some babies readily get into a sleeping, feeding, and changing routine, while others seem very unpredictable no matter how many tricks a parent tries. Some babies take readily to new events, such as the first bath or a new person, while others fuss and need more time to adjust.

These personality traits and others are unique to each child and tend to persist over time. An active baby, for example, may become the child who runs wildly around the house every time her friend comes to visit. The unpredictable infant may become the unpredictable toddler refusing to eat at regular meal times only to insist she's hungry one hour later. The baby who fusses when someone new takes care of her may later need some time to warm up to a new person or place.

Historically, problems seen in children were primarily attributed to the influence of the mother or other caregiver. In the 1940's and early 1950's, however, Drs. Stella Chase and Alexander Thomas began challenging this assumption. They recognized through their clinical practice that the personality of the child, *i.e.*, how the child behaved, was "either ignored, minimized or categorized as secondary" to the mother's attitude or caregiving practice. In 1956, these pioneering physicians began a longitudinal study to better understand this concept they called "temperament" or personality.

Over the past 30 years, numerous research studies have been conducted to isolate and understand the individual behavioral styles of children and their significance to the child's development. (*Temperament in Clinical Practice*, Stella Chess, M.D. and Alexander Thomas, M.D., The Guilford Press, N.Y., 1986) Today, temperament programs are in place at Kaiser Permanente for the prevention and early intervention of child behavior problems.

Temperament describes how a child behaves—not why or how well he or she behaves. Temperament won't tell you what is motivating your child to scream loudly when others barely let out a sound, nor will it tell you how adept your child will be at riding a bike or whether he will learn to ride sooner than your neighbor's child.

It's useful to understand your child's temperament to help a nanny know who your child is by how he behaves. Educating your nanny as to your child's temperament will help avoid an unfavorable match between a nanny and your child or an unfavorable perception of your child by your nanny. This knowledge may help your nanny understand, for example, that your daughter needs time to warm up to a new person and that her clinging to your skirt is not a sign that she doesn't like the nanny. Such knowledge may also help your nanny understand that your son expresses how he feels with a lot of intensity, regardless of whether his feelings are positive or negative—for example, he may scream with joy when she bakes his favorite dessert and he may scream and throw toys when he's frustrated.

Temperament (extracted with permission from *Temperament in Clinical Practice*, by Stella Chess, M.D., and Alexander Thomas, M.D., The Guilford Press, New York, 1986)

Infant Traits (0 - 12 months)

1. Activity Level: The motor component present in a given child's functioning and the diurnal proportion of active and inactive periods. *E.g.*, "She kicks and splashes so much in the bath that the floor must be mopped afterward," or "She can turn over but she doesn't do it much."

2. Regularity: The predictability and/or unpredictability in time of any function. It can be analyzed in relation to the sleep-wake cycle, hunger, feeding pattern, and elimination schedule. *E.g.*, "Nap time never changes no matter where we are, and he sleeps from two to two-and-one-half hours without fail," or "At feedings, sometimes she drains the bottle, but other times she's done after only two ounces or so."

3. Approach or Withdrawal: The nature of the initial response to a new stimulus, be it a new food, a new toy, or a new

person. *E.g.*, "He always smiles at a stranger," or "He ignores a new toy until it has been around for several days."

4. Adaptability: Responses to new or altered situations. *E.g.*, "When he first was given cereal, he spit it out, but it took only two or three times and he was eating it with gusto," or "Every time I put her into her snow suit she screams and struggles till we are outside—and that has been going on for three months."

5. Threshold of Responsiveness. The intensity level of stimulation that is necessary to evoke a discernible response, irrespective of the specific form that the response may take, or the sensory modality affective. *E.g.*, "If a door closes even softly, he startles and looks up," or "He can bang his head and raise a bump but he doesn't cry or change his behavior."

6. Intensity of Reaction. The energy level of response, irrespective of its quality or direction. *E.g.*, "When she is hungry she cries loudly from the beginning—there is no mild fussing at all," or "He had an ear infection and his eardrums were bulging but he behaved only slightly less frisky than usual and whimpered a bit."

7. Quality of Mood. The amount of pleasant, joyful and friendly behavior, as contrasted with unpleasant, crying, and unfriendly behavior. *E.g.*, "Every time he sees food he doesn't like, he whines and fusses until I take it off the table," or "If he is not laughing and smiling I know he's getting sick."

8. Distractibility. The effectiveness of extraneous environmental stimuli in interfering with or in altering the direction of the ongoing behavior. *E.g.*, "He likes to poke objects into

the electric outlets but his attention can easily be shifted by offering a toy," or "She has learned to push a little table around the house and if it gets stuck she cannot be side-tracked but keeps trying."

9. Attention Span and Persistence. Attention span concerns the length of time a particular activity is pursued by the child. Persistence refers to the continuation of an activity in the face of obstacles to the maintenance of the activity direction. *E.g.*, "Even though we can get him sidetracked by a toy, as soon as we stop playing with him he returns to his own task of poking at the electric outlet," or "If the bead doesn't go on the string immediately, she gives up."

Toddler Traits (12 to 24 months)

1. Activity level: *E.g.*, "When a friend from the nursery school comes to visit, [my daughter] immediately starts a game of running around wildly," or "Given a choice of activities, he usually selects something quiet such as drawing or looking at a picture book."

2. Regularity: *E.g.*, "Her big meal is always at lunchtime," or "Sometimes he falls asleep right after dinner and on other days he keeps going until 9 or 10 p.m.—there is no predicting."

3. Approach or withdrawal: *E.g.*, "We went to a new play group yesterday; as always she plunged right in," or "We started a new play group two weeks ago. Although it meets three times a week, he remained on the side for the first whole week and only last week did he begin to participate in activities."

4. Adaptability: *E.g.*, "She got her new tricycle and couldn't master it, so she called it stupid. But then I noticed her practicing on it every day and by a week she was out pedaling happily with her friends," or "It took him all fall to go contentedly to nursery school and each time he gets a cold and is out for several days, he becomes reluctant to go again."

5. Responsiveness: *E.g.*, "She likes her eggs scrambled one particular way; if they are a shade harder or softer she won't eat them," or "She never complains about feeling cold even though she may be shivering and her lips are blue."

6. Intensity: *E.g.*, "When I make him his favorite dessert, he jumps with joy and runs shouting to tell his sister," or "If another child takes her toy she grabs it back but doesn't cry."

7. Mood: *E.g.*, "She typically comes home from nursery school full of complaints about the other children," or "It's a pleasure to come home; she tells me all the nice things she did with smiles of enjoyment."

8. Distractibility: *E.g.*, "His room is strewn with toys; he scarcely has begun playing with one when his eye is caught by another and he keeps changing, forgetting to put anything back," or "If she decides she wants to go out to play and it's raining, she will fuss and won't accept any substitute."

9. Attention span: *E.g.*, "If he is pushing his wagon about and it gets stuck he struggles and yells until it moves again or else he comes for help. He doesn't give up," or "He asked to be taught to draw a dog but lost interest after the first try."

WORKSHEET:

MY CHILD'S PERSONALITY

How would you describe your child's personality?

What is a typical day like with your child?

What are your child's routines?

What are familiar interactions and how do you handle them?

What daily interactions with your child best describe each trait listed below? (*E.g.*, "My son squirms and kicks so much when I'm changing his diaper that it's impossible to get the diaper on. Only when I distract him by moving the blue bunny against the wall is it possible to finish!")

1. Activity level

2. Regularity

3. Approach or withdrawal

4. Adaptability

5. Threshold of responsiveness

6. Intensity of reaction

7. Quality of mood

8. Distractibility

9. Attention span and persistence

PUTTING IT ALL TOGETHER: SAMPLE INTERVIEW QUESTIONS

Here are sample interview questions covering the general areas discussed in this section. You should supplement these with questions specific to your family.

Always respect the information applicants provide about the children and families they have worked with. Recognize that an applicant's relationship with the children she has cared for is unique to her and for that period of time. These questions are intended to help you understand what an applicant knows about children, her caregiving style, orientation, and philosophy.

1. You took care of Johnny for some time. Can you tell us about him? How would you describe his personality?

2. Can you describe a typical day with him? How has this been different with other children and families you have worked with?

3. How did you help him learn to go to sleep on his own?

4. How did the feedings go? What did he eat, when, and how? What were the rules in the family around eating? What are yours?

5. How would you play together? What did he enjoy? What was he not interested in?

6. How did you help him learn new words? When did he begin to learn his words? How did he let you know what

he wanted when he didn't know the words? What seemed easy for him, when and why?

7. How did the temper tantrums go? When did they start, and how long before he outgrew them? What did you find worked best to help him out? Did you see eye-to-eye with the parents on this and why?

8. When did he learn to share things? How did he learn? How did you help him?

9. In a nanny's working relationship with parents, there can be difficult situations that come up which can be hard to talk about. Can you tell me about those you have experienced? How did you talk about them, and how were they resolved?

10. We all learn from the culture we grew up in what is important in life. How is it different growing up in your culture than here in the U.S.?

11. Can you tell us about your background? Where were you were raised? What type of work do your parents do? Do you have brothers and sisters? Your own children or grandchildren? How do you keep in touch, when and where?

12. Can you tell me one piece of advice that was handed down to you by your parents that reflects a value important to you and that you feel is important for a child to learn about the world?

iii.
the essentials

IMPORTANT CONSIDERATIONS

When Isabelle started everything was fine. The kids were happy and doing well. My only complaint was that the house was a mess! The afternoon dishes were still in the sink and the kids' toys were everywhere. I didn't have it in me to say anything. After all the kids were doing okay. I didn't want to rock the boat.—parent

When I started working for the family I thought I would just be taking care of the children. Then slowly over the next few months the mom kept adding housework. Pretty soon I was doing more housework than child care. I really didn't like it, so I quit.—nanny

Have you ever been asked by a friend to help out for a party only to find yourself fumbling around trying to figure out what she needed? You were in a bind. If you asked what she needed you to do, you seemed incompetent (after all, you should know). If you didn't ask, certainly you risked being incompetent (after all, your idea of helping out might not be hers)!

On the other hand, what if your friend asked you to help out and then slowly added more and more for you to do. You certainly were in a different bind. You agreed to help out but had no idea she expected so much. If you stopped, you ran the risk of her thinking you were not helpful at all.

Parents and caregivers can find themselves in the same kind of bind. Unless it's clear among everyone what is expected, misunderstandings are bound to occur and resentments soon to follow. In this chapter we look at *what* you want in a nanny as well as other issues that are essential to address before going any further in the process.

A job description is simply that—a way to describe what the job entails. Some parents, however, have a hard time knowing exactly what they want, particularly new parents who have not hired a nanny before. Do you want someone full-time or just two to three days a week? Do you want a nanny for your child only or to share with another family? Do you want your nanny to take care of the children and clean up the house? If you are a stay-at-home mom, who changes the diapers and who runs to the store for milk? Do you really need someone who drives a car if your child is now only three months old? But what will happen when an emergency comes up or when your child goes to preschool?

As you can see, the questions can be endless. Many are practical questions that can be answered quickly. In this chapter we'll look at all the pieces that go into a job description so you can decide about them before you get the word out to the universe that you are looking for a nanny. Equally important, we'll look at issues of immigration status, taxes, and other considerations that will affect the job description.

♥ Here's a note to note! If you're finding the easy answers don't come easily and the questions seem endless, then stop for a moment. If you think about what you're trying to do here, you'll realize that this job description is in fact the first written declaration to the world that you are leaving your child under someone else's care. The difficulty you are experiencing in writing the job description may be hiding a deeper worry. The real worry may be about separation. ♥

In general, you can expect a caregiver's primary responsibility will be to provide safe, predictable, and reliable care for your children. You can also expect that she will do the housework related to the children's care, such as making certain the children's room is clean, their laundry is done, and their toys are clean and put away. You can expect a caregiver will run errands as needed and if possible, and will keep your house in the same order in which it is usually kept (that means you don't come home to find your house in total chaos or so straightened up that you can't find anything!).

Anything else is gravy. If you want someone to take on more responsibility, such as having dinner on the table when you come home, you need to put this in your job description. If you don't, you'll find you'll be putting your nanny in the same kind of bind you were in with your friend who asked for some help during the party. You run the risk that when you ask your nanny to run to Safeway for milk she will think, "Oh yeah, milk today. I'll be scrubbing floors tomorrow!"

Listed below are other very important items to include in your job description. Remember: this is your working document. You will not put all of this information in an ad or notice for general knowledge! (Note that some of the topics below involve legal issues that are discussed more fully in the Legal Issues chapter of this book.)

SALARY RANGE AND BENEFITS

In the Bay Area, the salary range for full-time, live-in nannies is $1,500 to $2,500 plus room, board, and use of a car (if available). Live-out nanny salaries average $12 to $15 per hour with an upward trend toward $18 to $20. Doulas earn from $15 to $28 per hour depending on education and experience.

Benefits for full-time care can include two weeks of paid vacation after one year of employment, seven paid holidays (Christmas, New Year's, Thanksgiving and the day following, July 4th, Memorial Day, and Labor Day), use of a telephone during working hours (the cost of any unreasonably long toll calls and long distance calls are not included), travel expenses when traveling with the family, and medical benefits. (See page 190 of the Resources chapter for group plans and fees.)

NANNY TAXES

The Internal Revenue Service (IRS) requires that parents paying a nanny more than $1,200 in a calendar year deduct the appropriate taxes from her salary and pay employer-related taxes on her salary. Know, before starting your search, whether you will be paying your nanny "under the table" or doing things "above board"! You both may agree on a salary of $13 per hour, but your nanny may expect $13 per hour net after taxes (in her pocket), which means about $14.50 per hour gross (before taxes). Some parents have made the mistake of not making this point clear in the beginning only to find themselves having to make a very difficult decision, namely, either pay their desired nanny $14.50 per hour or let her go and start the search all over again! (For more information on your legal responsibilities to the federal and state government, see the Legal Issues chapter.)

IMMIGRATION STATUS: LEGAL OR NOT?

Many caregivers lack documentation to work legally in the U.S. The Immigration and Naturalization Service (INS) requires that employers of household workers (yes, you!) check certain documents to confirm that the prospective employee has legal status to work in the U.S.

If you choose to hire only those caregivers with proper documentation, be certain you put this requirement in any and all announcements and remind prospective caregivers that you will be checking for documents as a condition of employment. (For more information on INS requirements and documents see the Legal Issues chapter.)

DRIVING

If public transportation is not available where you live, it will be necessary for your nanny to have a car to get to and from work. In most parts of the Bay Area, however, public transportation is available, and the only concern will be its reliability. (This is where the dependability of your caregiver is very important, as she will need to give herself sufficient commute time.)

If you want your nanny to use her car in the course of her work, you need to be certain she has auto insurance with limits of liability at least equal to or greater than yours. This ensures that if she were in an accident the insurance company would collect on her policy and not yours. If she uses your car in the course of her work, be certain to add her as an additional driver.

If you want your caregiver to drive in the course of her work, be certain she has a valid California driver's license. Don't be fooled by someone saying she has an international license or a license from her own country. These are not recognized by the state. If your nanny is stopped by the police and hands over an international driver's license or a license from another country, she will be subpoenaed to appear in court for driving without a valid license, and the car she is driving will be impounded. The cost to recover the car will be at least $150.

CPR, FIRST AID, TB, & HEPATITIS

You should expect that a caregiver has current certificates showing she has attended an infant-child Cardiopulmonary Resuscitation classes (CPR) and a First Aid class. "Current" means within the past year. The applicant should bring a copy of the certificate she received upon completion of the class for you to retain in your records. Several places offer classes regularly and at a reasonable fee. Many parents end up going to their first CPR and First Aid class with their new caregiver.

You should also expect that a caregiver has tested negative for tuberculosis (TB) and be vaccinated against Hepatitis A. A caregiver can be tested for TB free of charge at any of the public health clinics in the San Francisco Bay area. Vaccinations usually involve a fee.

For a more extensive discussion of these issues see page 158; for CPR and First Aid classes and public health clinics, see page 187-189 of the Resources chapter.

OWN CHILD (BRINGS TO WORK)

Increasingly, women of young children are working as nannies. Some will want to bring their own child or children to work. Others make child care arrangements with relatives or family day care centers. You can expect that approximately 6-10% of calls you receive in response to an ad will come from moms with young children. You need to decide before sending out job announcements whether you are comfortable with this arrangement.

Some of the pros include having someone experienced care for your child, having a playmate for your child, and enjoying reduced costs. (Since your nanny benefits by bring her child with her, you will pay her less.) Some of the cons include your child not getting 100% of the nanny's attention, possible rivalry or favoritism, and the possibility of conflicts when either the nanny's child or your child is sick (does she stay home or come to work?). If a nanny has children she does not bring to your home, she herself may have child care problems or sick children requiring her to stay home.

Many caregivers are very adept at caring for more than one child at a time. At the very least, parents who are interested in this kind of arrangement should talk in detail with a caregiver about these issues.

HOW MUCH ENGLISH IS "ENOUGH"?

Along the way in choosing a caregiver you will meet people from other countries. Caregivers' ability to speak English will, therefore, vary. Many are fluent in English, others can understand more words than they can speak, and some will know only "the important words."

This question of language causes a lot of anxiety for many parents. How much English is "enough"? How will a caregiver's ability to speak English affect my child's ability to learn and use the language? Will I be able to understand what my caregiver wants or what she may be concerned about? Will she be able to understand me when I ask her to do something that is very important to me?

Although these questions are complicated to answer, at the very least a parent should expect a caregiver to have enough facility with English to handle emergencies when they come up and to communicate with the parent about what goes on during the course of a day. (See page 156 regarding medical emergencies.)

Many parents speak other languages. Many want their child to learn another language and feel it is an advantage having a nanny teach their child. Some parents with limited second-language skills learn over time how to communicate with their nanny so that the words are increasingly understood between them. (If problems in communication arise and you cannot find a bilingual person to help out, you can schedule a three-way telephone conference with an interpretation ser-vice. See page 190 of the Resources chapter of this book.)

BACKGROUND CHECKS

There was something about her I couldn't put my finger on but she seemed perfect in so many ways I decided to hire her. She signed an authorization for a background check. Her criminal records came back showing she had been convicted of armed robbery, and court ordered her not to use illegal substances! Now this is a stupid, stupid nanny. —parent

I don't care that she is undocumented. I don't care whether she bought her social security number for $100. I only care that she tells me the truth! —parent

All her ducks were in order from the beginning. We weren't surprised when the background check cleared. It was the final piece in the puzzle to make it all fit together. —parent

On June 8, 1983, Mary Beth Philips left her six-month-old daughter, Elizabeth, with a neighbor's nanny to attend a 90-minute graduate class at U.C. Berkeley. When she came back to pick up her daughter, she was told there had been "a little accident" and that Elizabeth had been taken to Oakland Children's Hospital, convulsing and in a coma. Elizabeth remained in a coma partially paralyzed for eight days. Both retinas had detached, leaving her permanently blind.

Three years later, Philips was stunned when Alameda County Superior Court Judge Martin Pulich convicted the nanny of a felony of child abuse yet sentenced her to only five years' probation and 2,000 hours of community service and imposed a $100 fine. To learn from her "mistake," the nanny was allowed to take a live-in position as a nanny for another family!

Partly as a way to manage her outrage and complete horror that this or any other nanny with a history of child abuse could take care of children, Philips pounded on the door of every California legislator and urged them to create a better, safer system for children. It took 11 years, but Philips, along with Bonnie Reeves, a Fremont mother whose baby shared the hospital room with Elizabeth, succeeded. In 1994, TrustLine was formed.

TRUSTLINE AGENCY, (800) 822-8490

TrustLine is administered by the California Department of Justice and is under the jurisdiction of the Department of Social Services. TrustLine runs criminal and child abuse background checks on nannies to determine whether there are any substantial allegations of child abuse and neglect on the nanny's record and whether there are any convictions or a pattern of arrests without convictions in the State of California. TrustLine will also run a FBI check on a nanny to determine whether she has been convicted of felonies or misdemeanors at the federal level.

Once a nanny has cleared TrustLine, she is registered. TrustLine records are updated regularly. If a nanny tells you she is TrustLine registered, you can call TrustLine at (800) 822-8490, Mondays through Fridays from 9 a.m. to 5 p.m. and receive verbal and/or written confirmation.

Over 30,000 applicants have been investigated by TrustLine. Around 6-8% do not clear. These include convicted felons, murderers, rapists, and child molesters! These are nannies who provide fingerprints knowing, but probably denying, they will get caught. (This number doesn't include nannies who do not go through the process either because they refuse to give authorization or because the parents don't ask for it.)

If your nanny doesn't clear TrustLine you will only be told she doesn't clear. You won't be told why. Rest assured it is serious enough that you don't want this nanny taking care of your child!

What is the downside to TrustLine? It can take 6-8 weeks (possibly less) to clear an applicant. Since most parents need child care sooner, your nanny may be taking care of your children when you get notice she doesn't clear. Your anxiety level may go "through the roof."

What You Need to Know About TrustLine:

1. TrustLine reports only substantial allegations of child abuse and neglect. Although it determines what is "substantial," its criteria are extensive and cross-referenced.

2. TrustLine reports only that an applicant did not clear. It will not report why.

3. It can take 6-8 weeks to process an application (a month longer for FBI). That means you may find out two months after hiring your nanny that she didn't clear.

4. You need a signed release and fingerprints from your nanny to begin the process. TrustLine provides the release and forms. To expedite the process, a nanny can go to specified location and send fingerprints electronically. Call TrustLine for locations.

5. Applicants need an Alien Registration Card (green card) or California driver's license to register.

6. Fees are $130.

Is there a way to fill this 6-8 week gap? Fortunately, there is.

PFC INFORMATION SERVICES, (510) 653-5061

PFC Information Services is owned by Lynn Peterson, a former owner of a nanny placement agency and a concerned parent. PFC Information Services provides employee background checks for many corporations around the country and also conducts background checks on nanny applicants.

PFC Information Services will check:

1. Criminal records per court or jurisdiction in each state for felonies and/or misdemeanors.
2. Department of Motor Vehicles (DMV) records in every state for suspensions, license revocations, and moving violations. This is of critical importance because a DMV report can point to substance abuse problems (*i.e.*, DUIs).
3. Credit Report verifying an applicant's prior addresses and employment, as well as excessive debts or collections.
4. Social Security Scan verifying that the social security number is valid and verifying former addresses and employment.

What you need to know about PFC Information Services:

1. Nannies must provide a signed authorization to run a background check. Call PFC at (510) 653-5061, Monday through Friday, 9 a.m. - 5 p.m. for the appropriate forms.
2. A background check from PFC can be completed in 2-3 business days.
3. PFC can run a criminal and credit check on your undocumented nanny using a date of birth.
4. PFC has a 5-7% "hit" rate (meaning 5-7% of individuals

checked are found to have substantial items of note on their records).

5. Your nanny may have committed a crime in a county other than the one for which you ran the check.
6. Your nanny may have committed a crime under a different name.
7. Fees range from $15 - $40 per item checked or $95 - $135 for a complete profile.
8. A report documents exactly what is in the court records.

Lynn Peterson is conscientious and informed about the different types of checks and provides a lot of support and information to concerned parents.

Many parents use PFC Information Services to supplement TrustLine (since they check different indices) and to "fill in the time gap" before TrustLine is complete.

Always let an applicant know during the prescreening process that you expect her to authorize a background check. It will then be seen as a condition of employment rather than an indication that you have suspicions about her.

Finally, be aware that many nannies have been gainfully employed for years and have never been asked to have a background check. Be sensitive to her concerns as well as yours.

Am I required to disclose what I know?

Federal law requires anyone requesting an investigative report from a job applicant to inform the applicant of any information in the report that prevents an offer of employment. The person who sought the check must notify the applicant of the reason not to hire, send a copy of the report containing the derogatory information, and provide information about how the applicant can dispute it. An applicant has the right to dispute the information contained in the report. The applicant must contact the agency running the report within five days and notify the agency of her intent to dispute and then send a letter noting the same within 10 days.

Should I disclose what I know?

Some parents choose to stick their heads in the sand and deny what they know about a nanny. It is difficult and painful to disclose derogatory information to an applicant and worse, to have to disclose it to someone already working in your home. Your formerly "ideal" nanny may not act ideal during the process. Some parents are surprised to hear their nanny deny what is obvious, saying "It wasn't my fault" or "The police booked the wrong person." Some parents worry about retaliation.

As easy as it may be to stick your head in the sand about what you've learned, remember the single most important reason to disclose is to let the applicant know the seriousness of the work she has asked to do and to prevent her from working in child care ever again.

What should I do if my nanny commits a crime while I employ her?

If your nanny is arrested on criminal charges, you should cooperate with the investigating police officer to provide whatever information they need to process the charge. Immediately, tell your nanny she is not to return to your home or have contact with your child. You will stay in touch with the investigating officer, and if the allegations are shown to be incorrect, you may reconsider your decision. Do not return calls pleading for understanding, sympathy, or reconsideration.

Report the incident to Child Protective Services in your county so that the incident will show up on TrustLine reports should your nanny seek employment in child care in the future.

Remember:
You do not want other parents to unknowingly hire a nanny you fired because she was a danger to your child!

Is the playing field even?

Many applicants are legitimately concerned that the "playing field" is not even with respect to background checks. A parent gets to check into private aspects of a nanny's life, but nannies don't have the same information about the parents.

Many nannies have found themselves working for parents who have problems in the areas of substance abuse, domestic violence, finances, child abuse and neglect, or who have poor driving histories. Nannies always face the risk they will be poorly treated on the job. If your nanny brings up this concern, you may want to "level the playing field" by giving her authorization to conduct a background check on you.

WORKSHEET: JOB DESCRIPTION

A. Ages and number of your children:

B. Hours and days needed:

C. Flexibility:
      1. To work additional hours (weekends/nights)
      2. To provide 24-hour child care
      3. To travel with our family
      4. Other: _____
              _____

D. Care giving duties required:
1. _____ F/T or _____P/T care of my children, including maintaining their daily routines, taking them for walks daily, reading, singing, and playing with them, and stimulating their development.

2. Housekeeping related to their care, including laundry, cleaning their room daily, and making certain their toys are clean and put away.

3. Other: _____

_____

_____

_____

_____

_____

E. Household duties required:

    1. Keeping the house in the same order in which it is usually kept.

    2. Running errands as needed and mutually agreed upon.

    3. Other: _____

       _____

       _____

F. Salary range and benefits

- $_____ per hour $_____per month
- Taxes deducted? ___yes ____ no
- Room and board: __ yes __ no
- Car: ____ yes ___ no
- Vacation per year: one week ___ or two weeks___

- Seven holidays per year
- Medical insurance? __ yes __ no
- Sick days: ____ per year
- _____

G. Legal status
___ Must have legal right to work in U.S.
___ Prefer legal right to work in U.S.
___ Need not have legal right to work in U.S.

H. CPR, First Aid, TB, Hepatitis A/B/C
- Required?

I. Own child(ren) she brings to work
- Not a problem
- Depends of age/sex/personality of child(ren)

J. Language ability in English:
___ Fluent
___ Limited speaking ability okay if she understands
___ Sufficient if she knows the most important words
___ Not important that she speaks English

K. Speaks other language: _____ preferred

L. Car necessary:
- To get to your home
- Drives her car in course of her work
- Drives my car in course of her work

PUTTING TOGETHER A JOB APPLICATION

I hate paperwork!—parent

I don't have the time to send out applications ... I need someone tomorrow!—parent

I didn't get applications back from nannies I was very interested in hiring so I called them. They said the application was too formal and wanted too much personal information. Some nannies had taken other jobs while I waited for the application to come back. I think, in general, it's a good idea to have one for every nanny, but the trade-off is missing some potentially good ones.—parent

I talked to the mom on Monday, and she said she would be sending me an application. I got it in the mail on Tuesday and sent it right back. On Thursday I met with the family, and they hired me by Friday for a 'trial period.' I think the application made it a lot easier and told me they respected me as a professional.—nanny

When I got the application I was stunned! They wanted all this information about me. Not only would it have taken me a long time to fill it out, but this is the kind of information I only discuss in an interview because it's so personal. I decided I didn't even want to apply.—nanny

Applications are a great way to organize all the pieces of information you need to have on a nanny. They also, however, formalize the process in a way that may make some nannies feel uncomfortable.

I advise using them, but be creative in how you get the information. When you decide a prospective nanny is someone you want to know better, let her know you will be sending an application and job announcement to her. Let her know that you understand that this is something she may not have had to do in previous employment situations. Give her the chance to let you know whether she has any concerns about completing the application; if she feels strongly that it is too complicated or too personal, you can decide to go ahead and interview her without the formal application and get the information during the interview. In either case, whether you receive the application back before the interview or during it, be certain you gather the information for each applicant. It will help you evaluate potential applicants, give you questions to ask during the interview process itself, and act as a checklist to gather important information and documents before hiring.

The application includes general questions about a caregiver's background, child-rearing philosophies, and knowledge about children of a particular age. Anything more than this can be overload for an applicant; some parents, however, like to include some "How would you handle this?" questions as a way of knowing an applicant's specific child-rearing skills. The only caveat in including too much information is that it may deter an applicant from applying or predispose you to making a premature judgment about an applicant based on her writing skills.

(To obtain an electronic copy of this document so you can revise it, send an e-mail request to info@pince-nez.com.)

Child Care Provider
Application Form

Today's date: _____

Your name:_____

Address:_____

Telephone no.: _____ Fax no.: _____

Date of birth: _____ Place: _____

Marital status: ___ Married ___ Single
                 ___ Divorced ___ Widowed

Children? Yes ___ No ___

If yes, ages: _____

Social Security no.: _____

Name, address and phone number of the closest relative
living near you:

       Name:_____

       Address: _____

       Phone: _____

Address and telephone number of someone we could
contact in case of an emergency:

       Name: _____

       Address: _____

       Phone: _____

Your driver's license number: _____

State/country: _____ Expiration date: _____

Driving history (accidents, tickets, etc.):

_____

_____

Have you ever had a background check conducted?
__ Yes __ No
If Yes, with which agency? _____
If no, would you be willing to have one done?
__ Yes __ No

Have you obtained CPR and First Aid qualifications
within the past year? __Yes__ No
If yes, please attach certificates showing dates.

Health insurance company, if any:
_____

Describe any health problems that could affect your work:
_____
_____

Date and results of last TB test:
_____

Dates and results of last Hepatitis test:
_____

Dates of Hepatitis A and B vaccinations (if any):
_____

Medications you currently use:
_____

Do you have any relationships or involvements that would
interfere with making a work commitment of at least a year?
__Yes __No
If yes, please explain:
_____
_____

What are your salary and benefit expectations?

$_____ per hour $_____per month

Weeks vacation per year _____

Medical insurance: Yes_____ No _____

Room and board: Yes _____ No _____

Holidays per year _____ Sick days: _____ per year

Please attach a resume or list below all jobs, dates of employment, and job responsibilities

<u>Start Date</u>   <u>End Date</u>   <u>Employer</u>   <u>Responsibilities</u>

1.

2.

3.

4. References: Please provide at least three who know about you and your child care experience:

1)   Name: _____

       Address: _____

       Phone: _____

  2)   Name: _____

       Address: _____

       Phone: _____

  3)   Name: _____

       Address: _____

       Phone: _____

Why do you want to work with children?

_____

_____

What did you like most and least about the work?

_____

_____

_____

Describe the type of family you like to work for. What would the parents and the children be like?

_____

_____

_____

_____

What would you expect a child of 18 months to be learning about his world?

_____

_____

How would that change at age two?

_____

_____

_____

Please tell us about your experience in getting to know the children you are caring for. Have there been any unusual challenges along the way? If so, please tell us about them.

_____

_____

_____

_____

_____

As both your employer and someone who would welcome you into our home and family, we would like to get to know you better. Please tell us about your background. You might want to include where you were born, your parents' occupations, names and ages of your brothers and sisters, what schools you attended and for how long, what subjects you studied and your interests/hobbies. In summary, include any information that gives us a picture of you. You may use additional pages as you need them.

_____

_____

_____

_____

_____

_____

_____

_____

_____

_____

_____

_____

_____

iv.
the search

WHERE DO I FIND A NANNY?

Where's the best place to find a nanny if you don't have much time? — parent

Where can I find someone who has experience with twins? — parent

My son has been diagnosed with ADHD (Attention Deficit Hyperactivity Disorder) and needs special care. He needs a teacher, nurse, grandmother, and a saint all wrapped into one person! Is there a hot line to heaven? — parent

Does Mary Poppins read the Domestic Help Wanted ads in the San Francisco Chronicle? — parent

If you want to find the best nanny, go to the nanny placement agencies. — parent

If there's a general rule about where to find a nanny in the San Francisco Bay Area it's to decide the route you want to take and to knock on every door along the way—you never know who will answer!

The best nannies aren't necessarily sitting in the nanny placement agencies waiting for you to drop by with your checkbook firmly in hand. Warm, loving, responsible, reliable, and experienced nannies look for jobs in the newspaper, on bulletin boards, by talking with friends, and on the Internet.

HOTLINES, BULLETIN BOARDS, ADS, & WEB SITES

If you're a parent with unusual requirements, such as needing care for multiples or for a child with special needs, attend a meeting of your local support organization (such as the Marin Mothers of Multiples), and get the word out that you need child care. Then publicize your needs through bulletin boards and newspaper ads making sure you specify that you need someone either with experience or with an interest in caring for twins, a child with special needs, etc. ("experience with twins preferred"). There are many caregivers who have such experience. Don't be discouraged by your circumstances.

Remember that the greater the exposure your ad or announcement gets, the greater number of applicants you will have to choose from. Run a four-day ad in the *San Francisco Chronicle* (Sunday - Thursday) and neighborhood newspapers. Make one trip to a community bulletin board. Put a notice on the community college web site. This "package" should yield 40-50 responses within a week. Among these, approximately four to six callers should meet your basic requirements.

We're very lucky in San Francisco Bay Area! At our doorstep are people from all parts of the world looking to provide child care. We're also fortunate to have many universities and colleges providing Early Childhood Education courses for students. There are parenting agencies with community bulletin boards that caregivers check when looking for work. And, of course, there are newspapers, the main ones being *San Francisco Chronicle*, *Marin Independent Journal*, *Oakland Tribune*, *San Mateo Times*, *Palo Alto Weekly*, *Contra Costa Times*, and *San Jose Mercury News*. We also have community papers distributed to neighborhoods and to special interest groups, such as the Russian and Asian communities.

If you want a nanny from outside the Bay Area, you can place an ad in the local papers of the town or city in which you are interested. Some parents want a nanny with Midwestern values and run ads in the local papers there. Other parents look for nannies from other countries with values similar to their own. If you do go beyond the San Francisco Bay Area looking for a nanny, you'll need to do some thorough checking over the phone and then provide travel expenses (including a return ticket if your nanny doesn't match your expectations). Be aware of the risk. Nannies from solid Midwestern families also pierce their body parts, dye their hair orange, and miss their boyfriends back in Kansas!

In general, the cost to run an ad in the newspapers ranges from $55 - $135 per week. Bulletin board notices and web site ads can be placed free of charge or at a nominal cost.

Locations of bulletin boards and newspapers throughout the Bay Area and web sites are listed on pages 177-184 of the Resources chapter of this book.

NANNY PLACEMENT AGENCIES

I simply don't have the time to do this. —parent

I signed on with a placement agency and then placed an ad in the local paper. The agency sent along information about the same nanny who responded to the ad! It was an expensive lesson about the market. —parent

You may be first-time parent faced with the difficulty and worry involved in finding a trustworthy nanny for your baby. You may read this book and feel overwhelmed by the process of choosing a nanny. You may be an overextended and exhausted parent without the time to find trustworthy nanny. You may have had a bad experience finding a nanny on your own. Consequently, you may choose to go to an agency.

There are many different types of companies that provide nannies for families. These include placement agencies, employment agencies, "temp" agencies, and child care referral agencies. As the demand for in-home child care increases, more companies are entering the market, many of which address a particular need for families.

Some agencies specialize in temporary, "on-call" nannies sent to families on an as-needed basis. Others specialize in baby nurses or doulas. Employment agencies often establish a market niche such as supplying nannies from the Midwest. Some companies that traditionally supplied household help, such as maids and chauffeurs, have expanded to include nanny placement. The Internet has also played a role in expanding resources for nanny searches; it includes web sites that charge parents a registration fee to view applicant descriptions.

Placement agencies recruit applicants, check references and credentials, and gather documents to support an applicant's work history and experience. This information is passed along to parents for their review. If a parent is interested in a particular applicant, an interview is scheduled, and the parents proceed to interview the applicant until a decision is made to hire.

"Temp" agencies send prescreened nannies to families to cover temporary child care needs. Most often, the parents need someone to fill the gap until a permanent nanny can be found or until their full-time nanny returns from vacation. Agencies that place baby nurses or doulas also fit into this category.

Agencies make their money when they match a nanny with a particular family. It is becoming more common for agencies to charge a non-refundable fee to register. Most agencies charge their fee when a nanny is placed. The fee is either a pre-determined flat amount or a percentage of a nanny's annual salary. Others, including "temp" agencies, add a dollar amount to a nanny's hourly rate.

In addition to recruiting and placing nannies, agencies play a crucial role in educating parents about the market and about what expectations are realistic. Parents who expect a "Mary Poppins" to land at their door and perform unlimited tasks at any hour of the day or night for $10 per hour need advice in readjusting their expectations.

Just as there are no regulations governing who can provide in-home child care, there are no established guidelines to govern the conduct and credentials of nanny placement agencies.

Not all agencies are created equal. They vary considerably in the type and quality of services provided. Parents are therefore advised to ask meaningful questions before signing on with an agency (examples are included in the end of this chapter).

As the demand for child care increases, the complaints against placement agencies increase. Many complaints raise legal and ethical questions. Complaints have included situations where competing agencies call a nanny at work to offer her a "better" job for a higher salary. Other agencies, in an effort to maximize the likelihood of placing a desirable applicant, send a nanny to several families, creating a bidding war and thus a higher placement fee for the agency. A rare, highly unethical agency tactic is to place the same nanny over and over again with different clients, just after the refund period has expired with each family.

Parents need to be aware of what agencies can't do as well as what they can do. Primarily, they cannot provide what many parents want: a guarantee that the agency applicant is the most qualified and best available nanny. Agencies don't have exclusive access to the best nannies. Qualified nannies use all resources to find a good family to work with including community bulletin boards, local newspapers, and placement agencies. Also, some qualified nannies refuse to work with placement agencies after having had an unfavorable experience in the past, such as an agency being more interested in a placement fee than in finding an appropriate match between the nanny and the family. Some nannies also complain of having been sent to too many families or of being inadequately informed of the working conditions or expectations of the parents.

It is also wise for parents to recognize that a ream of paperwork about a nanny is no substitute for a parent's own knowledge about who can be trusted and who would be a good fit. A nanny with all the right pieces of paper can nonetheless be a disaster for a particular family.

Remember:
You are the expert about who is the best fit.

It's wise before contracting with an agency to ask meaningful questions. Here are some to consider:

1. What are the agency's actual fees? Some agencies charge a non-refundable fee to register. To place or send a temporary nanny or doula, some agencies charge a daily fee based on either a percentage of your nanny's hourly rate or a flat daily rate. For full- or part-time long-term care, most agencies charge a percentage of your nanny's annual salary or an amount equivalent to six weeks of her full-time salary. That can translate to $3,600 - $7,000, or higher for a full-time nanny.

2. What types of nannies do they typically place? How long do they stay with the families once they are placed?

3. What salaries do their nannies earn? What benefits are considered standard?

4. How large is their pool of available applicants? How long will it take before you begin to meet any?

5. How much screening they do for health, safety, and knowledge about children? What information do they provide from references?

6. What background checks do they run on their applicants

and when? Please note that California law requires placement agencies to process all applicants through TrustLine. An agency, therefore, must receive fingerprints from an applicant and send them to TrustLine. It does not mean an applicant has cleared—only that she is in the process.

7. What services does the agency provide to help you interview, choose, and negotiate for the best nanny for your family?

8. What is their policy for a nanny who is wanted by two of the agency's clients? Agencies send nannies to several families. What would happen if you wanted to hire the nanny another family wanted, but you interviewed her first? Many parents end up in a bidding war over a nanny, inadvertently benefiting the agency, which then gets a higher placement fee.

9. What follow-up services do they provide? What is their replacement policy?

See page 194 of the Resources chapter for descriptions of Bay Area nanny placement agencies.

WORKSHEET: POSSIBLE LEADS

Who do I know who might be aware of a good nanny?

Parents of children entering preschool or K?

Friends who employ nannies?

Friends/acquaintances moving out of area?

People who work with families? (Drs., nurses, teachers, etc.)

Where have I seen ads for nannies? (Church? Gym? Dr. office? Community bulletin board? Neighborhood newspaper? Grocery store bulletin board?)

_____

_____

_____

v.
the selection process

PRE-SCREENING

*Inevitably, the calls came while I was in the middle of something!
The baby would be in the kitchen sink happily splashing around,
my entire upper body soaking wet, soap suds dripping off my
elbows and the phone would ring. Another applicant was calling
about 'the job.' I felt frustrated and yet hopeful. I couldn't talk now
and couldn't get to a pen and write a number to call later. This is
a great introduction, I would think ... and then realized, 'Yes, it's
just what the job is about!'* — parent

*If I heard one more time, 'You need babysitter?' I would scream!
Where is my ideal nanny?* — parent

*It was so soothing to hear her voice describe her experience with
children. It was what she said and how she said it that made me
want to know more. This was the start I had hoped for.* — parent

There may not be a perfect time to pre-screen applicants, but
there certainly are better times! Once you've gotten the word

out and calls start coming in, inevitably you'll hear from applicants at all times of the day and night. Most likely you'll be in the middle of the daily routines—feeding or changing the baby, the kids running in and out of the house slamming doors, and the dog barking because he was left behind! If it's at all possible (most parents roll their eyes at this suggestion) set aside a quiet time to return calls. This is most easily done by using a designated line to take messages or renting a voice mail box for a month. You should plan on 15 minutes per call if you get a "live" person on the line.

Prescreening is exactly that. You want to weed out those applicants who do not meet your basic criteria from those who do. The first step in doing this is listening to the messages that come in. Listen not only to what they say but how they say it. Is her message clear? Is her facility with English adequate for your needs? Try not to set your standards too high. Remember many applicants feel anxious about leaving the "right" message. They know they are being evaluated and their anxiety may come across as hesitation, mumbling, or being curt.

Before you pick up the phone to return calls, be certain you have your job description and a pad of paper in front of you. You'll be taking a lot of notes and then transferring information about your most interesting applicants to the job application form you prepared earlier.

When you do get an applicant on the line, check to be sure that this is a good time for her to talk with you. If so, tell her you would like to let her know about the position to see if this is something she would be interested in. Then describe to her your job description. You may want to start by saying:

"Hello, my name is The Ideal Mom, and you had called me about The Ideal Nanny position I advertised in the Chronicle. Is this a good time for you to talk for a few minutes? I'd like to tell you about the position and see if this is something you would be interested in. I need someone to come to my home Monday - Friday from 7:30 a.m. to 6 p.m. where your responsibility would be to take care of my three-month-old son. I would also want you to keep the house in the same condition it is usually in and run errands as needed. I'm needing someone to start in three weeks. It is also necessary you have documents to show you can work legally in the U.S. and that you are willing to have the appropriate taxes deducted from your salary. Is this something you would be interested in?"**

If the applicant says yes, then ask her to tell you about her experience caring for children, including the dates she worked, the families she worked for, the ages of the children, and her responsibilities.

Now that's expecting a lot! Most nannies are not sitting in front of their resumes. Many have never put one together. As you know, many nannies provide professional, quality child care. They don't (nor does our society) consider their work "professional." For this reason, you can expect an applicant to describe in a loosely-arranged way her work experience. You'll need to ask questions to arrange it in a way that looks like a resume.

If you like what you hear and how you hear it:

1. Let your applicant know that as a condition of employment you expect she will have attended **CPR/First Aid class** within the past year, to have tested **negative for TB,** and to be **vaccinated against Hepatitis.** Reassure her that you will help her arrange for this.

2. Let her know you would need her to give you authorization to have a **criminal background check** done. Be certain she understands about the background check, since she needs to sign a release for you to have one run. (Letting her know now rather than later in the process can prevent her perceiving your request as a personal affront.)

3. You will then ask for the names of three people you could call as **references**. Expect that at least two are people she has worked for in the past. Others can be personal or character references. Some parents have had the experience that applicants don't know how to get in touch with any of their former employers (saying the families moved out of town or that she has lost their phone numbers). You should consider this as an indication of problems with former employers that couldn't be resolved or that the "employers" didn't exist. For this reason, don't consider the applicant further.

If you are not interested in the applicant, thank her for her time, and let her know you will be contacting her by the next day if you want to continue your discussions with her.

If you are interested in the applicant, let her know you will be calling her references and getting back to her by the next day to schedule an interview. If she doesn't hear from you she'll know you are not interested in considering her application. That way you don't need to return calls you either don't want to make or don't have time to make.

Congratulate yourself if you have gone through the above and have found a good applicant. You've completed an important piece in the process!

CHECKING REFERENCES

One thing that sticks in my mind about her is that she was like part of the family. She was there in the good times, sad, bad, and worried times. I even went away to Europe and left my son with her and I wouldn't do that with anyone. — parent

She gets down on the floor and plays with the kids. They love it. But it's hard for her to pull away when they're in the middle of it all. I usually come home to a house full of toys, glue, paper, scissors, and dishes left in the sink. She's great with the kids, but if you like a neat house she'll drive you crazy. — parent

She stole money from me, and she's not allowed back into this house! — parent

"She didn't have good role models with her own parents and hasn't made good choices in her personal relationships."-A reference for a caregiver who was seriously considered but later found to have been court-ordered into drug treatment and never fully recovered

If you have had a good introduction to an applicant, you're probably anxious to know as much about her as you can. References are windows into the world of the unknown. They can be like the controversial "Nannycam" (more about this in Chapter VII showing you this person day in and day out going through the routines of child care.

Before running to the phone, consider for a minute the dilemma some parents face after contacting references. Imagine you hear from one reference that the caregiver was "warm, nurturing, loving, and responsible." The reference couldn't say enough wonderful things about her. You then call the next reference who says the opposite. How can you evaluate someone based on two different opinions of her? The difficulty in these and similar situations lies in what you may be expecting to get from a reference. Many parents are looking for a "Good Housekeeping Seal of Approval" from a reference. They want reassurance they have found their Nanny from Heaven. But be aware that people providing references may have complicated motives for describing their former nanny in the way they do. (Or may be wary about giving criticism for fear the nanny may find out and sue for libel.)

One reference who gave a very curt, matter-of-fact description about her previous nanny admitted she was upset with this nanny for leaving, even though she conceded that she would have quit had she been in the nanny's shoes. The parents had been going through a rough divorce for over a year; they had cut the nanny's salary and were anticipating a move which would increase the commuting time for the nanny. The nanny had given six-weeks' notice prior to leaving so the family could find a substitute. In spite of all this, this mom had desperately wanted the nanny to stay and her departure still left her feeling abandoned.

Another reference (from a solid Midwestern state) gave a nanny a strong recommendation and failed to mention the nanny's cocaine use. Why? Because the employer and her husband also used cocaine—with the nanny! They did not see it as drug "abuse."

What should you expect to learn from a reference?

Remember:
You are a parent talking to a parent about inviting a
complete stranger to come into your home
and take care of the most important person
in your life.

Rule out risks to your child by asking these questions:

1. Any indications of abuse of alcohol or prescription drugs or use of illegal substances?

2. Anything in the way she responded to your child that caused concern—being overly harsh, punishing, or critical to your child, hitting, hurting or harming him in any way?

3. Anything in her personal life that interfered with her ability to pay full attention to your child when under her care?

Remember:
You should always ask the
rule-out questions to every reference. If you
get any response that does not reassure
you unequivocally that the answer is "no,"
then continue to ask questions until you are reas-
sured. If you are not, then rule out the applicant and
move on.

Most references are delighted to talk with you about their previous nanny. You can expect to hear an outpouring of warmth when the working and personal relationship has been supportive and satisfactory. You can also expect a realistic appraisal of a nanny's strengths and where she will need some help. It's up to you to go beyond the warm outpourings of affection and ask questions that will give you a realistic picture of the nanny's character and child rearing skills.

Can you ask personal questions about an applicant, such as how old she is, whether she is married and has children or even whether she has problems with alcohol or drugs?

Federal anti-discrimination laws apply only to employers hiring more than seven employees; similar state laws apply to those hiring five or more. Since most parents are not in that position, they can (and should) ask important questions into an applicant's personal life. (One caveat here: Your municipality or county may have enacted their own antidiscrimination laws that could prohibit a wide range of things. It's best to check first with your city/county attorney's office in this regard before beginning the interview process.)

Some questions are best answered by the applicant. These are questions about family background, medical history, etc. Some questions are best answered by references. These are questions about substance use and abuse and child abuse or neglect.

Be sensitive in the way you ask applicants for personal information. Remember you want to get a picture about who they are by learning about their personal life. You are not an investigator looking to solve a crime!

Be direct and succinct in asking references about substance use and abuse and child abuse or neglect. Wait until the end of your discussion before asking these questions. You may want to preface them by saying, "What I am about to ask is in no way a reflection of what you have told me about Mary but something I ask of every reference ...."

FORM: REFERENCE QUESTIONS

Here are some areas you can inquire into:

- Verify dates of employment, ages and number of children cared for, duties and responsibilities.

- Did the children like her? How long did it take for her to get to know them? Did the children feel she understood them? Did the parent feel she understood the children?

- Was she reliable and responsible? Was she on time or out sick very often?

- Did she use good judgment?

- Can you describe her character?

- How did she let you know when she had questions or concerns about the children and/or her relationship with you?

- How did she go about her duties? Did she need a lot of direction or take initiative?

- What were her reasons for leaving?

- Did she give you enough notice?

- Would you re-hire her?

THE INTERVIEW PROCESS

The first applicant who rang the bell was greeted by my daughter who told her, 'I don't like you, you're ugly ... go away!' She left and never called us again. —parents of a spirited two-year-old who had played Nanny Roulette too many times.

The first time I saw her I thought 'Oh my God, what's an oversized Winnie the Pooh tee-shirt doing on a 57-year-old oversized woman?' Within the hour I had fallen in love with her. She wouldn't win a beauty contest but she got straight A's in my book for knowing about kids. —parent

Over the phone she said all the right things. Her references said all the right things. During the interview she said all the right things. We didn't hire her. She didn't feel right. —parent

Our ideal applicant walked out on us to take a position with another family. We interviewed three others who couldn't match up to this 'ideal' person we had let slip through our fingers. When Doris came that day we were still hurting. She asked to hold the baby, and then we just talked about babies, about us, and about her while she walked and comforted our daughter. I'll never forget this strong sense of knowing she was 'right.' What she said was right. How she said it was right. Maybe she also helped us get over the loss of the ideal. —parent

I think parents and caregivers have to fall in love with each other. —nanny

Meeting a nanny applicant for the first time can be like a blind date with all the hopes, wishes, and preconceptions involved. After all, you've done your homework. You know what you want. You've also talked to this person on the phone about some of the most important details of her personal life and talked to others who knew her well. Now you're meeting her for the first time.

Most likely you have a picture in your mind of what she looks like. You already may have evaluated her in terms of your ideal based on what you know about her. You want this to be "it" and hope that by the end of the day your child care worries will be over.

Perhaps you've prepared ahead of time for the interview. You have all the important questions neatly typed on a piece of paper under the heading "The Agenda." Her application sits nearby carefully placed so your critiques and comments aren't visible. The baby sleeps soundly in the other room. You are poised and ready.

You may not be at all like the family above. Life in your house may be more hectic. Perhaps you have similar expectations and hopes but chaos rules and this evening is no exception! Most likely just as the doorbell rings announcing her arrival, your sweet-tempered child is learning how to "self-soothe." She's screaming for something, and you don't have a clue what she wants. The dog barks as if the house is being burglarized, and you're scrambling around trying to find those papers with all the important questions to ask written on them. Life is normal. You are not ready.

Whether you're the parent behind Door #1 or Door #2, you open your front door and meet this "wished-for," "hoped-for," "not-to-sure about" nanny face-to-face for the first time. You open the door to greet your ideal nanny and ... she doesn't look ideal at all. In fact she looks human. Your spirits drop and you wonder, "Is this the one with whom I'm going to trust my child? Where is my ideal nanny?"

Of course, the situation could be entirely different. What some parents experience at first is better than they imagined. Some parents begin by not expecting much. Perhaps they've been through it so many times that they hold any and all hope at arm's length. They take a wait-and-see approach. After all, a first meeting is just that.

The first interview is an important one. At the end of the chapter are some ideas about what you can expect to discuss and learn from the interview and what questions to ask. It is important, however, to keep in mind that this is one interview, a "first date," and others should follow. Don't pressure yourself into making a final decision by the end of the first interview. Give yourself time to meet a second, third, and even a fourth time.

Many parents are legitimately concerned that if they wait to decide about hiring a good nanny she will be scooped up by another family. If you find after your first interview that the nanny is someone you are very interested in hiring, let her know that you are very serious and want to schedule a second interview. Let her know that you expect she is also interviewing with other families and would want to know if she is in final negotiations with any of them. Give her permission to tell you she has another offer! You are then both in a position to proceed in an informed and timely way.

If you went through the worksheets at the beginning of this book and at the end of this chapter, you have spent a good deal of time evaluating what you need in a caregiver. You put together questions to ask in an interview and know what answers to listen for. You have a picture in your mind of someone who would be ideal. You have an idea of what characteristics she would have to make her fit into the rhythms and routines of your family life. You know what your child-rearing philosophies and style are. You know who your child is developmentally and his idiosyncrasies.

You certainly should have a lot to discuss with a caregiver. But now that she's here you may be wondering: Where and how do I begin?

No two interviews are alike, and no two people are alike. For that reason, it is impossible to proceed with a strict agenda. A parent should expect, however, to accomplish the following in the first interview:

1. **Clarify the expectations of the position.** Go over the job description with the caregiver to be certain you both understand what the hours, days, responsibilities, and conditions of employment are.

2. **Go over with the caregiver what you know about her personal and work life.** Ask her to fill in what is missing and to correct what is wrong. Be curious about her life experiences and ask her questions that help you understand how those experiences influenced her decision to work with children and how she works with children. Remember your questions about cultural differences! Think with her about the advice and values questions that you answered. Make note of how these affect how she responds to children in particular situations.

3. **Discuss her child care experience and philosophy by asking about the children she has cared for.** As she describes who they were, listen for her understanding of children's different temperaments. Listen for her understanding of what the child would be doing at that age. Talk

about your child in terms of the same areas. Ask those questions you put together earlier, such as "What are your thoughts on feeding on demand or on schedule? Was Matthew fed on demand? Did you ever need to change that so he could get into a regular schedule? We're in that position now with Sophie. What have you tried that worked?"

4. Give her permission and an opportunity to ask questions about your child, your family, and you as a parent.

5. End your first meeting by revisiting the conditions of employment, *i.e.*, CPR/First Aid classes, TB testing and the background check. Review important documents, such as her driver's license and request those that are missing.

6. Let her know you will be contacting her by the next day to discuss how you will proceed. You will both need time to "sleep on it." Be certain she knows that she can call you with questions at any time.

FORM: INTERVIEW QUESTIONS

Can you tell us what your experience has been taking care of children?

What motivates you to care for children?

How would people who know you best describe you?

Can you tell me about the children you cared for?

How would you describe their personalities?

How did this make a difference in how you cared for them?

Please tell us about your background (where born, parents' occupations, names and ages of brothers and sisters, what schools attended and for how long, what subjects studied and interests/hobbies).

What important values did your parents teach you?

Describe the type of family you like to work for. What would the parents and children be like?

Other questions:

_____

_____

_____

_____

_____

_____

_____

_____

vi.
legal issues

LEGAL ISSUES

We use the 'don't ask, don't tell' policy in our family.
Documentation is way down on our list of priorities.—parent

In our family, it is very important we comply with all the rules
and regulations. When we hired [our nanny] we checked her
documents and began deducting the appropriate taxes from her
salary. Three months later she told us she bought her social
security number in the Mission for $100! We felt furious, betrayed
and then had to start all over again.—parent

I learned the hard way that an international driver's license is not
legal if someone is in the U.S. more than 20 days. [Our nanny]
was driving our kids for months before she was stopped for
something minor. The police impounded her car and issued her a
subpoena to appear in court for driving without a valid license. It
was devastating for everyone.—parent

When she said she wanted $13 an hour, she meant $13 an hour in her pocket. That meant $14.50 an hour with taxes. The difference meant we couldn't afford her. — parent

In the U.S. today, everything seems complicated by legal issues. Hiring a nanny is no exception. As many parents will remember, Zoe Baird lost her chance at high public office because she failed to pay taxes on her nanny's salary.

Parents are responsible to numerous federal and state agencies when hiring a nanny: At the federal level, the Internal Revenue Service (IRS) and the Immigration and Naturalization Service (IRS), and at the state level, the California Internal Revenue Service, the California New Employment Registry, the California Worker's Compensation Department, and the Department of Motor Vehicles (DMV).

IMMIGRATION AND NATURALIZATION SERVICE

For generations, people from all over the world have emigrated to the U.S. for political, social, and economic reasons. We are selective in how wide and to whom we open our doors to accept them. As the economic disparity grows between the U.S. and other countries, an increasing number of immigrants come to the U.S. to make a better life for themselves or to support those they have left behind. These include well-educated professionals as well as unskilled laborers.

Because the market for in-home child care is unlicensed and unregulated, many immigrants without documentation for legal employment work in the U.S. as nannies. They answer ads in newspapers, post notices on bulletin boards, and ask friends to help them find work. They include teachers, nurses, lawyers, physicians, students, accountants, and parents with many years' experience raising children and grandchildren.

Legal status is not an indicator of quality! It is, however, an indicator of risk to both parents and caregivers. You should know the risks before you start your search because it will affect the salary you pay, whether a nanny can drive your children, and what risks you will face if caught.

People who believe hiring undocumented workers is wrong, who hold or have a chance to hold a public office or a high profile position, or who are otherwise subject to public scrutiny, will want to be certain they hire a nanny with documentation to work in the U.S. and pay the appropriate taxes.

Fines for hiring an undocumented nanny are assessed when the INS comes knocking on your door, and you don't have a completed I-9 form signed by you and the nanny. This form can be downloaded at www.ins.usdoj.gov. Or call (800) 375-5283. Civil fines for noncompliance are approximately $350. Criminal charges can be made if a parent is found to have brought a nanny across borders illegally or to have altered documents. Your nanny (and her family) may be subject to deportation.

INTERNAL REVENUE SERVICE

It is vital that you decide whether you will be paying taxes on a nanny's salary before you start your search. If an applicant wants $13 per hour in her pocket that means $14.50 out of yours! The difference could make a big difference in your child care costs.

The IRS requires parents who pay a nanny $1,200 or more in a calendar year to pay the appropriate federal and state employer-related taxes. Parents must withhold FICA (Social Security) from a nanny's pay and report this withholding to the IRS quarterly or at year-end. In addition, parents must pay employer taxes at year-end on the monies paid to their nanny that are reported on Schedule H of their tax return. Parents are not required to withhold federal or state income taxes from their nanny's salary. The payment of these taxes can be the nanny's responsibility when she files at year-end.

The amount of employer-related taxes paid at year-end depends on your tax situation. All or part of these taxes can be recovered at year-end by taking a child care tax credit and by using pre-tax dollars from a flexible spending account set up by your employer.

Parents' tax responsibilities and available credits are outlined in detail in Internal Revenue Service Publication 926, which can be downloaded at www.irs.ustreas.gov. Since tax laws can be extremely complicated, parents should consult with their tax accountant regarding how hiring a nanny will affect their own tax situation. A web site, www.4nannytaxes.com, calculates the amount of withholding and employer taxes on a gross salary. Your accountant can set up the accounts necessary to comply with tax laws. Alternatively, you can have payroll accounts established through third party providers such as Breedlove & Associates or Paychex. Telephone numbers and web site addresses are included at the end of this chapter.

The IRS will assess penalties and interest on unpaid taxes if you are audited.

Many parents do not pay taxes on child care because it increases their already high cost of care and because the accounting system can be time-consuming to set up. The IRS has also been lax in tracking parents who do not pay taxes on child care since it is simply not cost-effective for them to do so. If you decide you will not pay taxes on child care, consider it wise not to "double-dip." Taking a child care tax credit or using pre-tax dollars to pay for child care and then not paying taxes is most certainly a red flag to the IRS!

STATE OF CALIFORNIA "NEW EMPLOYMENT REGISTRY"

The state of California requires all new employers to report information about new employees to the New Employment Registry. This is the state's way of tracking "deadbeat dads." To obtain the form call (916) 657-0529.

STATE OF CALIFORNIA WORKER'S COMPENSATION INSURANCE

The state of California requires parents to provide worker's compensation insurance for their nanny. Otherwise, parents can be sued by their nanny for an on-the-job injury. Worker's compensation insurance can be obtained by putting a rider on an existing homeowner's or tenant's insurance policy at a nominal annual cost. A nanny must work at least 52 hours or earn at least $100 in 90 calendar days to qualify. Since this is private insurance, legal status is not a condition of eligibility.

CALIFORNIA DEPARTMENT OF MOTOR VEHICLES (DMV)

If your nanny drives your vehicle, she should be added to your auto insurance policy as an additional insured driver. If the nanny uses her own car, she should have liability, property damage, and medical coverage at least equal to the coverage limits of your own policy. This will help protect you if the injured party sues you for an accident your nanny caused, wholly or in part, while working for you. If at all possible, see if your nanny will also have you added as an additional insured on her policy. These measures will provide two layers of insurance coverage for you in the event of a claim or lawsuit.

Parents should note that anyone residing in the U.S. longer than 20 days is required to have a valid California driver's license in order to drive in California. Penalties for driving without a valid license include impounding the car and issuing a court appearance notice to the unlicensed driver. An international driver's license or a license issued in the nanny's country of origin are not considered valid. Fees for impounding a car in San Francisco include $100 towing fee and $30-$50 per day storage fee. The car must be recovered by the registered owner.

The Department of Motor Vehicles has made it quite difficult for someone without legal status to obtain a California driver's license. In October, 2000 the DMV began running social security checks to ensure the social security number given by an applicant belongs to the applicant (social security numbers bought illegally no longer work).

Here are the DMV requirements:

1. U.S. birth certificate or passport with INS form I-94 attached verifying legal status to remain in the U.S. and dates permitted to stay;
2. Social security number;
3. $12 fee; and
4. Passing score on a written/vision test and/or driving test.

Parents can verify that their nanny has a valid California driver's license by having her bring a copy of her DMV record. DMV records can be obtained from any DMV office for a $5.00 fee. Parents can purchase a copy of the California vehicle code from the DMV to interpret citation codes which may appear on a caregiver's record.

For further information contact your local Department of Motor Vehicles.

EQUAL EMPLOYMENT OPPORTUNITY COMMISSION

Employers hiring fewer than seven employees are exempt from federal antidiscrimination laws and those hiring fewer than five employees are exempt from similar state laws. This means you can and should ask any and all relevant questions about an applicant to ensure she provides safe, reliable, and responsible child care for children (*i.e.*, history of drug and alcohol abuse, child abuse and neglect, criminal record, family history, etc.). (Before you delve into this, however, make sure your county and city have not passed any applicable antidiscrimination laws.)

OTHER LEGAL MATTERS

If your nanny takes care of a child other than those she is employed to take care of, and that child is injured while in her care, you can be sued for negligence for either not having used good judgment when hiring or not having provided adequate training to prevent the injury from occurring. In essence, your best friend can sue you if her child is injured while in the care of your nanny!

IMPORTANT TELEPHONE NUMBERS

- Immigration and Naturalization Service, (800) 375-5283
- California New Employee Registry, (916) 657-0529
- Internal Revenue Service, Federal Household Employment Tax Laws, Publication #926, (800) TAXFORM (www.irs.ustreas.gov)
- California Employment Development Department for California Household Employment Tax Laws, (415) 929-5700
- California Department of Motor Vehicles, Customer Service Department, (415) 557-1179
- California Equal Employment Opportunity Commission, (415) 356-5100
- To calculate taxes paid to caregiver: www.4nannytaxes.com
- Payroll tax accounting systems to pay taxes for a nanny: www.4nannytaxes.com; Paychex, (650) 952-5777, www.paychex.com; Breedlove and Associates, (800) 723-9961

iii.
the contract

THE CONTRACT

If you had insisted on a contract, I would have gone somewhere else. —caregiver

Unless these things are clear ahead of time and in writing, I know I'll end up just like before where I'm doing more and more and then leave feeling resentful and upset at myself for getting in that position. —caregiver

I want to leave it informal. We've already talked about what she's supposed to do and how much she's getting paid. —parent

The relationship you have with your nanny is complex. Most certainly it is unlike any other working relationship you have ever had before! On the one hand, clearly you are an employer hiring an employee to perform certain duties during certain hours and days for a set fee. On the other hand, you are inviting someone to come into your home and take care of the most important person in your life. Your employee's duties and responsibilities are, for better or worse, intricately interwoven into your personal and private lives.

Day in and day out your employee feeds, bathes, and dresses your child, plays with her, and helps her get to sleep. Day in and day out she sets limits, guides, and teaches your child about what is important in life. She lets you know what your child did and said. You discuss what occurred during the day and why. You and your nanny simultaneously wear different hats, so to speak, namely, a professional hat and a personal hat. It can be subtle, but the hats you both wear can change imperceptibly. Many a parent has found herself sitting across the kitchen table from a nanny who seems more like her best friend, her grandmother, or her sister than an employee. Many a nanny has found herself in a similar situation.

THE EMPLOYER-EMPLOYEE RELATIONSHIP

All parents walk this fine line in their relationship with their nanny—the line between the professional and the personal. Some are more adept than others in keeping this line clear in their minds and moving between their two roles. They can turn to their nanny for advice when they are worried about their child's behavior, feeling as if she was their beloved grandmother—and knowing she isn't. Other parents are not so adept at this. Much of the time the nanny feels like grandma or mom's best friend. For these parents, it's much more difficult to keep the boundaries clear.

It is not the parents alone who walk this fine line. Nannies also walk it. As can be expected, some are better than others in keeping the line clear. Sometimes, nannies ask parents for favors that go well beyond what employees typically ask from their employers. These favors may include legal assistance to obtain working papers, money to pay a debt, or even help finding a new employer! Other nannies want emotional support and advice. Many parents have found themselves on the phone late at night or even on weekends offering advice and support to a nanny who is ending a difficult relationship with her boyfriend.

These boundary violations can be subtle. It is not always clear either where the line should be drawn or even how to draw the line. What works in one relationship may not work in another. One parent who paid off a nanny's debt engendered such loyalty and trust that the loan was repaid quickly, and the nanny provided responsible, loving care for many years after. Another parent who helped her nanny get working papers soon found herself without child care when her nanny went to work for another family who offered a higher salary!

Why should a parent notice this fine line? Because when parents need to talk with their nanny about something that has to do with their professional working relationship, the concern can be dismissed because the relationship seems personal. In the routine of daily life, it can mean that when a parent comes home every night and the dirty lunch dishes are still on the table she may find it easier to clean up the dishes than to remind her "grandmother" that it is her responsibility. It could be a more complex situation—like saying yes to paying off a debt when good judgment may indicate otherwise, or staying up night after night advising a nanny when good judgment would suggest the nanny consult with a professional for help with difficulties in her personal relationships.

A working agreement is therefore important to help you and the nanny maintain the professional and employment aspects of the working relationship. It provides a concrete starting point for the parent and the nanny. Such an agreement sets the stage for a parent to say, "Tamara, I'm going to take off my hat where it feels like you're my grandmother and put on my hat where I'm your employer. We need to sit down and talk about the fact that the dirty lunch dishes are on the table every day when I come home." Or "Dominique, I'm going to take off my hat where it feels like you're my best friend and put on my hat where I'm your employer. I think you need to talk with someone professionally about your difficulties with your boyfriend. It's best for everyone."

Is it necessary to put a working agreement in writing? Not necessarily. Some parents and nannies are more comfortable with a verbal agreement. Other parents and nannies want a formal, written document. What is most important is not what form it takes but that a formal discussion between parent and nanny takes place.

Also, remember that your nanny should be included in discussions about what goes into the agreement. That doesn't mean she makes the final decision about the terms, of course. That responsibility is for the employer. But it does mean your nanny should enter into negotiations with you about the terms of her employment.

BINDING OR NOT?

Most, if not all, working agreements between a parent and nanny are binding contracts which can be held up in a court of law. If your nanny, for example, walks out on you without giving adequate time for replacement, you can sue her for breach of contract. Likewise, if you fail to pay her salary, she can sue you for breach of contract.

What a working agreement can do is clarify between you and your nanny the terms of your working relationship: the hours, days, duties, salary/benefits, conditions for termination, etc. This gives both parties a clear understanding of what is expected of the other and something to stand on when misunderstandings or changes come up.

What should a parent include in the agreement? Certainly an agreement should include work hours, days, and responsibilities, as well as salary, benefits, and terms of termination. Many parents, however, overlook some other terms which have to do with the explicit or implicit "rules of conduct" of your family life. Consider these routine issues:

- Who is allowed to visit when she's working?
- Where is your nanny allowed to take your child?
- Who answers the phone? (Do you want your nanny to answer your phone when it rings or let the answering machine take it?)
- Where does the money come from to buy treats for the child or groceries?

Many parents find themselves clarifying these issues piecemeal as they come up. It can be as simple as "hands off the Toblerone chocolate" in the pantry or more complicated, such as where the nanny is allowed to take your child. One parent fired her nanny for taking her son to a boyfriend's home several times and then denying it. The child had not been harmed or injured during these visits, and the parent may have allowed him to go had introductions been made and permission obtained beforehand. But the discovery after the fact and the nanny's attempts to cover up created such suspicion and doubt that the relationship could not be repaired.

If you decide to hire a nanny who does not have much facility with English, it would be wise, after you put your agreement into writing, to have it translated into her native language. See page 190 of the Resources chapter for companies that provide translation and interpretation services in many different languages.

If the relationship deteriorates beyond repair and you find yourself needing to recover monies from a nanny to cover lost or damaged goods (or $800 in long distance telephone calls) you can always sue your nanny (by now, probably former nanny) in Small Claims Court. Parents can also bring a civil action for abuse or neglect, and, if successful, secure a judgment lien or wage assignment against a nanny.

Congratulations to both you and your nanny if you have come this far! This Working Agreement is one concrete way to clarify a very complicated relationship. It can get you both off to a good start as you continually sort through the complex relationship you have created!

WORKSHEET:

EMPLOYMENT AGREEMENT CHECKLIST

The following is a checklist of items that can be included in a working agreement. A sample working agreement follows. (You have to use your judgment in determining how long and how detailed to make the agreement. As in many other contexts, even the most sophisticated person can be offended when presented with a long, complicated legal document in fine print!)

<u>Working Agreement</u>

1. Terms:
- Beginning date of employment
- Ending date of employment
- Hours and days of work
- Predictable or rotating
- Flexible, as-needed
- Travel

2. Duties and Responsibilities:
- Related to child
- Related to housekeeping
- For child only

- Other, including errands as-needed
- Health and safety
- CPR/First Aid/swimming courses required
- TB, Hepatitis testing/vaccinations required
- Communication w/parent about child (daily/weekly/monthly)
- Transportation of child

3. Compensation

A. Salary

- Hourly/weekly rate of pay
- Overtime/holiday pay
- Travel pay
- Guarantee minimum hours
- Taxes withheld

B. Benefits

- Vacation
- Holidays
- Medical/dental
- Automobile
- Room/board
- Telephone
- Travel
- Meals

4. Termination

- Required no. of days for advance notice vs. "at will" employment
- Conditions for termination

- For employee
- For employer
- Trial period

5. Confidentiality
- Information learned about parents/child/family
- Information learned about nanny
- Areas of house to be kept private from nanny

6. "House Rules" or "Rules of Conduct"
   Visitors:
- Number of guests allowed during off-hours (1, 2, 3)
- Hours allowed to visit: __ working hours ___ off-hours
- Hour they are expected to leave by: _____
- Introductions necessary beforehand
- Opposite sex allowed
- Use of family quarters allowed by visitors
- Food/beverages offered
- Overnight guests allowed
- Prior consent required
- Visitors allowed during working hours
- Advance notice expected
- Relatives allowed to visit and stay

   Visiting Others
- Our child allowed in homes of others
- Advanced notice required
- Required they be known to us
- Allowed in homes with swimming pools

141

- Allowed in homes with pets

Food
- Food is allowed to be eaten in:
  - Kitchen
  - Dining room
  - Living room
  - Nanny quarters
- Special food requests are allowed, provided they are healthy and not overly expensive
- Clean up expected after food preparation
- Alcohol is/is not allowed and is/is not provided
- House is vegetarian/vegan/kosher/other

Nanny's Room
- Dirty dishes/food must be removed from your room
- Personal decorating allowed (hanging pictures on wall, etc.)
- Moving furniture around allowed

Automobile
- Car should be cleaned once/month
- Oil checked once/month
- Gas tank filled when at 1/4 or other
- No driving when sick or on medications which interfere with judgment
- Unusual auto sounds or performance should be brought to our attention right away
- Extensive personal use of car requires fill-up at nanny's expense

- Accidents require police to be notified immediately then us. Never leave the scene of an accident.
- You are responsible for insurance deductible if accident is your fault
- Hit and run accidents are cause for immediate dismissal
- Seat belts are required for all passengers at all times
- Do not eat and drive
- Children in back seat at all times—never front
- Car seat to be used at all times, no exceptions
- The car must return home every evening, even if you don't return
- Pull over to use mobile phone

Telephone
- Take and record messages when possible and on pad near telephone
- Personal calls on our phone are allowed during your work hours only; otherwise please use your own phone
- Charges for long distance and/or toll calls made from our telephone will be deducted from your salary
- Mobile phone use

Money
- If you are short of cash and need an advance, please ask us
- Money in the emergency fund is for emergencies only (as described)

- Items purchased for the house from your funds will be reimbursed immediately. Receipts are necessary.

Privacy
- Confidentiality about our personal lives is required
- Bedrooms are off-limits unless invited (both ours and yours)

Personal Habits
- No smoking in house, car, yard, or around child
- No drinking of alcohol during working hours
- Driving and drinking is never allowed
- Illegal drugs are never allowed
- If you are sick, please let us know immediately
- Use customary manners, such as "please" and "thank you"
- Let us know if the temperature in your room needs adjusting
- Appropriate dress is required when out of your room
- TV watching in our living quarters is/is not allowed during working hours
- TV watching in our living quarters is/is not allowed during your off-hours
- Stereo playing at reasonable volumes in our living quarters is allowed during working hours
- Use of home computer is/is not allowed
- Child's use of computer/TV must be supervised

Emergencies
- Please provide the name and telephone number of nearest relative/friend to contact in the event of an emergency (and Dr. name, phone, and any medical conditions or allergies)
- If you will be away overnight, please provide a telephone number and address where you can be reached in case of an emergency
- Please let us know when you will be gone overnight.
- Please carry at all times during working hours the Emergency Medical Form for our Child
- Please carry your cell phone/pager at all times during working hours

Following on the next page is a sample contract that can be modified to reflect the specific agreement you reach with your nanny. To obtain an electronic copy, send an e-mail request to info@pince-nez.com. Please have a licensed California attorney competent in employment law review the sample contract and any modifications you make to it to ensure the contract's legality and enforceability and that it meets your specific needs. See page 190 of the Resources chapter for sources for having your contract translated into your nanny's native language ($220- $450 for translation into Spanish, 3-4 day turn-around).

Form: Employment Agreement

This employment agreement is made and entered into by
_____residing at _____,
CA (Employers) and _____ and
_____residing at _____,
CA (Employee), as of _____, 200__.

In consideration of the mutual promises made herein, the parties agree as follows:

1. **Term of employment:** Employment shall begin on
_____, extending indefinitely subject to the conditions
of termination described below.

2. **Duties:** Employee shall perform the following duties:

   Child care: Provide full-time care for Employers'
   child(ren), _____("Child/Children"),
   including but not limited to feeding, changing, bathing,
   providing developmental and educational activities, and
   looking after the health and safety of the Child.

   Household duties: Provide light housekeeping related
   to care of Child, including washing up dishes, washing,
   drying, and putting away baby clothes, preparing food for
   Child, keeping the nursery room and other play areas
   tidy, putting away toys, and any other household duties
   required to provide a high level of child care.

Communication: Communicate regularly and frequently with the Employers regarding health, safety, daily activities, development, and other topics related to child care.

Transportation: Provide transportation to and from specified activities (swimming, parks, etc.), as needed, as well as be prepared to transport Child to an emergency medical facility if needed. This duty is subject to proof of a valid California driver's license, a safe driving record, and adequate insurance coverage on the part of the Employee.

Errands and other miscellaneous duties: Employee will, in the course of other child care duties, from time to time pick up groceries, drop off packages at the post office, pick up laundry, or perform other reasonable errands and tasks, providing such errands and tasks do not interfere with the performance of child care duties, are performed during the regular hours of employment, and do not otherwise unduly inconvenience the Employee.

3. **Compensation:** Employers shall pay Employee a salary of $____ per hour for a minimum of ___ hours per week during the term of employment. Employee will be paid for any time worked in excess of ___ hours at the rate of $___ per hour.

- Employee shall be paid 33% of her hourly rate when providing care for Child during hours when both Employee and Child are sleeping.

- Employers will also pay the standard 50% Employers' share of Social Security, Medicare and Unemployment taxes. Employee shall be responsible for the balance of these taxes plus any applicable federal and state income taxes.

- Employee shall be paid biweekly for actual hours worked or for ___ hours per week, whichever is more, subject to deductions for time not worked in excess of vacation and holiday time as described below.

4. **Benefits:** Employee shall receive the following benefits:

Vacation/personal leave: Employee will receive ten (10) paid vacation days per year, earned at the rate of 5/6 day per month worked, commencing on the first day of employment. After the first 120 days of employment (4 months), Employee may borrow additional vacation days against future earnings. In the event that Employee terminates employment before taken vacation days are earned, they will be deducted from her final pay check. While not mandatory, every effort will be made to coordinate Employee's vacation with Employers'.

Holidays: Employee will receive seven paid holidays each year, including Christmas, New Year's, Memorial Day, July 4, Labor Day, Thanksgiving, and the day following Thanksgiving. Upon mutual agreement of Employer and Employee, Employee may work a given holiday in return for receiving an additional vacation or other personal leave day.

Time off during Employers' vacation: In the event that Employers take vacation that is not concurrent with Employee's vacation, Employee will be paid at the minimum rate of 20 hours per week, even though the Employee may not be required to work. During such periods, Employee may be required to visit Employers' home up to five days per week to feed pets, water plants, bring in mail, and perform other minimal maintenance duties.

Other paid time off: No other paid time off will be given without changes to this agreement by mutual consent.

Health insurance: Employee shall be reimbursed for personal health insurance in the amount of $____ per month, to be paid monthly.

Telephone: During working hours, Employee will have unlimited use of Employers' telephone for local calls. Unless agreed to in advance, long distance calls will be paid for by Employee through payroll deductions.

Travel expenses when traveling with family: Employee will not ordinarily be expected to accompany Employers on overnight or out-of-town trips unless mutually agreed upon. In the event of such travel, Employers will pay all direct expenses related to such travel, including transport, meals, and lodging. Employee will be paid for actual hours worked or a minimum of ____ hours per day and will be expected to perform child care duties for that amount of time. During such travel, Employee may be asked to adjust hours to provide, for example, evening baby sitting in place of child care duties during the day.

Meals: Employers will provide adequate and appropriate food for Employee during normal work hours.

5. **Termination.** This Agreement may be terminated under the following conditions:
   a) By either party upon 30 (thirty) days' notice of the other party, or
   b) By Employers immediately within the first 60 days of employment, which period shall be considered a "trial" period if and when any of the following occurs:
      • Neglectful or abusive care of the child;
      • Frequent lateness or absence by Employee to work;
      • Blatant failure to perform duties as defined in this agreement;
      • Failure to follow "house rules" as described in Section 6 below, or
   c) Immediately by Employee if Employers fail to make salary payments within ____ days of the due date, grant the vacation days that Employee is entitled to take, and/or make reasonable efforts to protect the safety and well-being of Employee.

6. **Confidentiality:** Employee agrees not to disclose any personal, family, or other information about the Employers or Employers' family or household without the prior written consent of the Employers.

7. **House Rules:** Employers agree to abide by the following "House Rules" during working hours. These rules may be changed from time to time at the discretion of the Employers with a minimum 48 hours notice to Employee.

- Keep doors locked at all times when at home.
- Close and lock all doors and windows and set alarm whenever leaving house.
- Do not smoke, drink alcohol, or take illegal drugs.
- Limit personal phone calls to reasonable and necessary local non-toll calls.
- No TV during the day unless previously agreed to by Employers; only radio or recorded music that is mellow or otherwise appropriate for children.
- Never leave Child unattended for any reason.
- Do not open the door to anyone unless they are expected visitors or individuals known to both Employers and Employee.
- Contact either Employers immediately in the event of any problem, including but not limited to health and safety of Child, safety and security of the house, and health and safety of Employee.
- Notify Employers immediately in the event that Employee is injured in any way.
- Do not invite others to the house or visit others' homes with Child unless agreed to in advance by Employers.

In witness whereof, the parties hereto have executed this Employment Agreement as of _____, 200__.

Employers: _____

_____

Employee: _____

vii.
health & safety

HEALTH & SAFETY OF YOUR CHILD

One of the primary responsibilities you hand over to your nanny is to protect the health and safety of your child. She should, therefore, be knowledgeable and competent to handle medical emergencies as well as the expectable "bumps and bruises" of a child's daily life. If your child chokes on a piece of food or falls off the swing and breaks his leg, you want your nanny to act quickly and knowledgeably. Other relatively routine experiences, such as cuts and bruises, should also be handled competently and quickly. Before you allow a nanny to begin working for you, make sure that the following areas have been covered.

MEDICAL EMERGENCIES AND PREVENTION

Before leaving your child with your nanny for the first time, be certain you have posted a list of names and contact numbers of people who can be reached in a medical emergency. Don't put the list in a drawer or on a cluttered bulletin board! Your nanny may not find it when she needs it.

Review with your nanny how you want her to handle emergencies when they come up. If her English is limited be certain she can do the following:

1. Dial 911
2. Tell the person who answers:
   a. Address (house number, street, city, and cross street)
   b. Telephone number (including area code)
   c. Number of people injured
   d. Names of the children injured
   e. Ages of the children injured
   f. Nature of the emergency (burn, broken bone, can't breathe, choking, heart stopped)

It's not a bad idea to keep posted next to each telephone in your home your home phone number and your address (with cross street) in case your nanny has to give this information to the fire or police department in an emergency situation when she may be in a panic. If you have an alarm system, involve your nanny in choosing a code and password that she can easily remember (such as her anniversary date and childhood pet's name rather than yours).

DISASTER PREPAREDNESS

Because the Bay Area is at high risk for earthquakes and mud slides it is wise to review with your nanny the procedures for handling these disasters. Be certain she knows (1) where the Emergency Disaster Kit is located, (2) where flashlights are kept, (3) where to take the children in case of a disaster, and (4) how to contact you.

FIRE SAFETY

Your nanny should know the location of and how to use the fire extinguishers and smoke detectors in your home. She should also know the best escape routes from your home in a fire and how to find them if there is thick smoke. If she stays overnight, be certain she keeps a flashlight by the bed and that she and the children keep thick-soled shoes under the bed (to prevent injury when walking over broken glass).

INFANT-CHILD CPR AND FIRST AID TRAINING

As mentioned in Chapter III, as a parent you should expect your nanny to have current infant-child Cardio-Pulmonary Resuscitation (CPR) training and First Aid training.

According to the Red Cross, caregivers should have an initial CPR and First Aid training course followed by annual refresher courses to keep skills current. These classes are generally eight hours long and given in one full day or two separate evenings. The fees average $80 for both. A list of locations appears on page 187 of the Resources chapter.

You should be certain your nanny completes or has scheduled this training prior to employment. If she has recently attended, be certain she brings a copy of her certificate with her for the first interview.

Parents may want to have a monthly review with their nanny on the above emergency procedures (CPR/First Aid, disaster preparedness, and fire safety) so everyone is prepared, knowledgeable, and competent to handle them when they happen.

TB TESTING AND HEPATITIS IMMUNIZATION

Many parents overlook requiring a nanny to have tested negative for and have immunizations against highly-contagious diseases, such as Tuberculosis (TB) and Hepatitis.

Tuberculosis is a highly contagious and life-threatening disease that had been held in check in recent decades but is lately showing a resurgence worldwide. In November 2000, the World Health Organization reported that 40% of the population of Southeast Asia is infected with the disease, which caused 1.9 million deaths there in 1999.

In a survey of 25 caregivers in San Francisco, 60% of respondents reported they had never been tested for TB! While this may not reflect the population at large, it is a warning sign which parents should heed. You should be certain your nanny has tested negative for TB (via a simple skin scratch test) and ask her to give you a copy of the test prior to starting employment! All individuals working in day care or schools (even parent volunteers) are required to test negative for TB.

Hepatitis A is considered by the Public Health Department to be epidemic in San Francisco. It is contracted via food and fecal matter. Hepatitis B is often contracted by teenagers and young adults (including through piercings and tattooing). It can lead to cirrhosis and liver cancer. It is spread through cuts and scrapes, body fluids and sexual contact.

The U.S. Centers for Disease Control strongly recommends infants be immunized against Hepatitis A and that everyone under 18 be immunized against Hepatitis B. Immunization requires a series of vaccinations administered over a several-month period. Your child may have received the vaccination as part of his or her routine immunization program.

Child care workers in both family day care homes and day care centers are required to be vaccinated against Hepatitis A. It would be wise for parents to consult with their pediatrician for his or her recommendation about vaccinating a nanny against Hepatitis A and B!

Hepatitis C is a disease of the liver and is spread primarily through contact with blood. There is no vaccine to protect against it. For more information on Hepatitis A, B or C see www.cdc.gov/ncidad/disease/hepatitis.

Public health clinics in the Bay Area provide free weekly testing for TB. Some clinics also provide vaccinations against the Hepatitis A and B virus for $125 - $150 per vaccine. Parents should consult with their neighborhood public health clinic or their physician regarding the Hepatitis vaccines.

A list of public health clinics appears on page 188 of the Resources chapter.

FORM: MEDICAL TREATMENT CONSENT

Date: _____

To Whom It May Concern:

We, _____ and _____
(Parents) hereby give permission to_____
(Nanny) to authorize emergency medical treatment for our
child, _____ . Such treatment must be
provided by a licensed physician, hospital, emergency
medical facility or qualified medical staff.

_____   _____
(Parent's name)   (Parent's name)

_____   _____
(Parent's signature)   (Parent's signature)

_____   _____
phone (work)   phone (work)

_____   _____
phone (mobile)   phone (mobile)

_____   _____
pager   pager

vii.
How do I know if my nanny is doing a good job?

YOU'VE HIRED A NANNY: NOW WHAT?

She's a cut above the rest! Anything we can do for her we'll do. —
parent

*They have a secret world between them I can't enter. On Saturday
mornings my daughter will get exasperated that I don't know
which bowl she eats her favorite cereal in. Or she'll say something
only she and Myrna understand. I've given up trying to know
everything that goes on around here.* —parent

*She wants to be part of the family. In her mind that means the
freedom to know every detail about our private lives.* —parent

*My daughter says she hates her but she came so highly
recommended. Should I fire her?* —parent

She's very knowledgeable, reliable, and responsible but not the warm and fuzzy type. I wonder if my kids need warm and fuzzy. Lately, I've been window shopping for another nanny. I see warm and fuzzy nannies everywhere. Is my head not on straight here??—parent

Congratulations on hiring your nanny! You've completed a tremendous project and made one of the most important and meaningful decisions in your family's life.

Now what? What do you need to know about managing the complex task of caring for children in partnership with your nanny?

There is absolutely no formal research to date investigating the complex relationship between parents, their children, and the nannies the parents hire. You can assume, however, that many of the same considerations involved in keeping other employment and personal relationships healthy are equally applicable to the nanny-parent-child relationship.

One thing that should be avoided in the nanny situation in particular is the "I want what she has" approach! What works for one family may not work for you. It can be very tempting to try to recreate the seemingly ideal relationship your best friend has with her nanny. However, the relationship nannies and parents create is unique to each family. Understanding your relationship with your nanny is essential to making it work.

The following guidelines should help in beginning the relationship on a healthy note and helping identify and solve problems that may arise.

BASIC NEEDS TO KEEP THE RELATIONSHIP HEALTHY

1. **Trust.** At the most basic level, you must trust that your nanny would not deliberately cause harm to you or your child.

2. **Communication.** If you want to keep the relationship active and ongoing, talk openly and regularly about:

    i. What goes on between your nanny and child during the day;

    ii. Your working and personal relationship with her;

    iii. How she is managing her personal life.

3. **Respect for privacy.** It would be devastating to find your personal life aired in public, equally so for your nanny. Both you and your nanny must keep confidential what you see and hear about each other's personal lives and know where to draw the line about what each is entitled to know.

4. **Ideas and opinions.** What your nanny has to say about your child and her relationship with you has a lot of meaning and value. Remember to keep an open mind as to personal and cultural differences.

5. **Education and training.** All professionals expect ongoing education and training to keep skills current and ideas flowing. Your nanny is no exception. (See the Nanny Education, Training, and Support discussion on p. 170.)

BAND-AIDS CAN'T SOLVE THE PROBLEM

Always try to see what underlies an unusual or unexpected request from your nanny or changes in her behavior. If your nanny asks for time off, a change in hours, more pay, or if she is consistently late, always leaves the dishes in the sink, or forgets to call when expected, don't ignore the change. Although you may choose to grant the request or accommodate the behavior, always try to explore and address the "why."

GLITTER AND GOLD ARE ONLY WINDOW DRESSING

Don't fool yourself into thinking that allowing your nanny to live in your beautiful home, take exotic vacations with you, and receive top dollar will keep your nanny happy. Children, including yours, can be demanding and exasperating as well as intriguing, emotionally satisfying, and tremendously interesting. Staying alone for hours with a tantruming toddler in a four-star hotel can be exasperating and lonely, even if it is the Ritz Carlton in Paris!

RESPECT THE CONTRACT

Adding, changing, and rearranging terms without a clear agreement between you and your nanny is a setup for disaster. Nannies leave when small things add up.

Make sure you discuss with your nanny any desire you have to change the original agreement you entered into.

UNDERSTANDING THE SOURCE OF THE PROBLEM

- Is the problem a change in your child's behavior?

    Your child may be going through a different phase in development or adjusting to changes in his life.

- Is it a difference in understanding your child's behavior?

    You and your nanny may have a different understanding of why your child is acting a certain way.

- Is it a difference in how you are responding to him or her?

    You and your nanny may be responding to your child differently or inconsistently.

- Is this between you and your nanny?

    How do you feel toward her when she acts a certain way?

- Is this a change within yourself?

    Have your feelings changed about wanting or needing a nanny? Have your feelings changed about who you thought you would want?

- Has the situation changed?

    A move to a new home, a new baby, separation or divorce, a change in workload can place a strain on the relationship.

SHOULD MY NANNY GO?

1. **Evaluate the concern.** If your child says she hates her nanny, this statement isn't necessarily proof that the nanny is harming her. It may be your child wants the nanny to leave so you will stay home.

2. **Trust your gut, and know when to ask for help.** If your child regresses to an earlier stage in development, it may be a sign that something is wrong. Pay attention if your child is:

- Unusually withdrawn
- Overly aggressive
- Unable to make friends or get along with others
- Reverting to earlier behaviors she once mastered

In these situations you may want to seek professional help.

3. **Discuss your observations with trusted relatives and friends.** Talk with them about your concerns and seek out advice.

4. **Discuss your observations directly with your nanny.** Ask if she has observed similar changes. Talk specifically about what you know and do not know. Ask for help in resolving the problem.

5. **If, in spite of the above, your child's behavior continues to be difficult and serious, it may be necessary to ask your nanny to leave.**

WHEN YOUR NANNY <u>MUST</u> GO

1. Any indications of alcohol or drug abuse.
2. She is yelling at, hitting, hurting, or harming your child in any way.
3. She is neglectful and inattentive, particularly in situations that compromise your child's safety.
4. Driving recklessly when your child is in the car.
5. If allegations of criminal activity are made against her.

NANNYCAMS: THE HIDDEN INVESTIGATIVE EYE

"Nannycams" (surveillance cameras that come hidden in fully-operable clocks, VCRs, air purifiers, smoke detectors, and even teddy bears!) are windows into the world of a parent's deepest worry. Perhaps your child is acting unusual, and you have a gut feel that something is not right between your nanny and child. Your gut tells you to observe every nuance in their relationship for evidence that your child is being harmed.

Perhaps it is not your child, but your relationship with your nanny that seems unusually difficult. You may worry that it will "spill-over" and cause harm to your child, or you may look to your child's behavior as confirmation of the worrisome feelings you harbor towards your nanny.

Some parents choose to alleviate this unspoken worry by setting up a hidden video camera (which can be purchased or rented from various companies) to find the hidden "aha" they are looking for. With the evidence clearly documented, they can fire their nanny with conviction. Here are some pros and cons of using a Nannycam:

PROS
- You get a "private eye" to watch your nanny interact with your child.
- If your nanny is acting improperly, you have solid evidence with which to confront her.
- You can fire your nanny with conviction.

CONS
- Nannycams raise legal questions about a nanny's right to privacy vs. a parent's right to know.

- The camera only records what is directly in front of its lens.
- It can be non-reassuring if nothing is found.
- Your nanny can feel spied upon if she finds out you have videotaped her without her knowledge. The deception may be impossible to repair.

Sources for Nannycams are listed on page 191 of the Resources chapter of this book.

NANNY EDUCATION, TRAINING AND SUPPORT

All day long I'm home alone with the baby. I love him dearly and we've gotten very attached. But there are times I'm frustrated and bored. I would love to have a conversation with someone over the age of eight months! — The Stay-at-Home Nanny Blues

Most of the day we are out and about. It's good for the baby and for me. She gets fresh air, learns all the sounds, smells, and sights of the outdoors and to play with other kids. I get to see other nannies with their kids. We talk about ourselves, the kids, and help each other out when we need it. — The Neighborhood Nanny

I'm a nanny with strong Christian values. It's been hard finding other nannies with the same ideas. When I went on-line at the Nanny Network I met others like me. Now I'm part of a strong support group across the country! I'm wired and it's great. — The Dot.Com Nanny

She's been going to the park every day for the past two weeks. Yesterday she asked for more money or she's leaving. I know they're organizing down there! It's like a nanny union shop in the park. — The Worried Mom

There are several challenges nannies must negotiate when working with children and families. One of the greatest difficulties is managing isolation. Unlike caregivers in day care centers, nannies have no co-workers with whom to share their thoughts, ideas, and daily experiences. Even though nannies have plenty to do during the day, other adults are not always around to provide company. Your child gets sick, and they both must stay in for a week. You move to a rural neighborhood, and she has no car. You all go on vacation to Hawaii, and she's in the hotel room with the baby most of the day and night. Your darling two-year-old has a series of meltdowns, and your nanny needs support and new ideas from someone who is not necessarily you.

The isolation and recognition challenges are greatest for a live-in nanny who is new to the area. She needs to create a social network of friends while, at the same time, learning how to fit into the family's routines and understand the children for whom she is caring.

Another challenge for nannies is getting much-deserved recognition, education, and support for the important work they do. The recognition of nannies as early childhood professionals is abysmal in this country. Public policymakers, educators, and parents continue to refuse to treat nannies as professionals with a need for education, training, and support.

Unfortunately, only a handful of training programs for nannies exist in the U.S. These programs' stated purpose is to educate and train nannies, but one must question whether they can do this in the two to three month course that is offered.

The complexities of understanding the developmental needs of children, family dynamics, and the role of a nanny would best be served by long-term education by accredited teachers. Short-term training can be extremely useful, provided the students have the entry-level degree of maturity and previous relevant work experience to benefit. Most, if not all, U.S. nanny training programs fail in both categories. It is horrendous and a sad state of affairs to recognize that in the entire San Francisco Bay Area there is not a single accredited course or program in any university or community college designed for in-home child care professionals or nannies! As a result, nannies turn to each other to find the professional training, support, and recognition they need.

Sometimes nannies create a neighborhood group, either at the local parks or on-line, to be connected to other nannies on a daily basis (sometimes to the chagrin of parents who suspect price-fixing).

In 1981, Deborah Davis, Ph.D. recognized nannies' need for support. In a grass-roots way, she helped nannies meet regularly to discuss their common interests and concerns. Today this informal gathering of nannies has grown into an international organization, International Nanny Association, which publishes a bi-monthly publication, the National Nanny Newsletter. The success of the INA inspired others in 1992 to found the National Association of Nannies (NAN). NAN sponsors annual conferences with nationally recognized speakers who discuss current trends in child development, professional education, and child care legislation. NAN also sponsors a web site where nannies go on-line to meet other like-minded professionals for support.

The Bay Area Nanny Association (BANA) is NAN's regional partner supporting nannies all over the Bay Area with a current membership of 37 and growing. BANA members meet monthly for various social, educational, and community service events. Nanny organizations are listed on page 186 of the Resources chapter.

Each of these organizations is actively involved in getting national recognition for the education and training of nannies at accredited Early Childhood Education programs in community colleges and universities. They also seek recognition by professional organizations, such as the National Association for the Education of Young Children (NAEYC) and its affiliate, the California Association for the Education of Young Children (CAEYC).

Should parents be worried their nannies will unionize "in and out of the neighborhood park"? Does this mean the cost of care will rise? It may be hard to imagine that nanny collaboration means anything other than disaster for parents already worried about the affordability and availability of care-by-nannies. Yet socializing with other nannies can be a huge benefit to nannies who sing the "home-alone" blues or those who want recognition for the vitally important work they do. Such socializing also can be of benefit to parents in that it may increase the quality of in home child care. Ultimately both families and nannies benefit.

AFTERWARD

If you have read through this book before starting to look for a nanny, you should feel well equipped to handle the nanny search process. If you have already found a nanny through the advice given in this book, congratulations! You can go to work or address other responsibilities in your life knowing your child is being cared for by someone you have carefully screened and chosen.

Choosing a nanny for your child is one of the first big decisions you make about your child's daily care and guidance. More choices are in the future including preschool and elementary school. As you continue through the process of making these important decisions, you can use the research skills and insight about your child's development and temperament that you have used in choosing a nanny.

One last word of advice: Enjoy the relationship you have begun with your nanny and settle into the daily routines. But don't neglect the future. It's time to look into the preschool situation in your area and get on the wait list of any school you would like your child to attend!

Alyce Desrosiers, LCSW

xi.
resources

WHERE TO POST/PUBLISH NANNY ADS

Note that parents must post their own ads on community service bulletin boards. Call for hours of operation. Child Care Resource and Referral Networks provide information and referrals for available openings in child care centers or family day care centers. They can also connect you with sharecare, playgroups, and co-ops.

SAN FRANCISCO

Bulletin Boards
- Parents Place, 3272 California Street, (415) 563-1041
- Perinatal Education and Lactation Center, CPMC, 3898 California Street, (415) 346-BABY
- Natural Resources, 1307 Castro Street, (415) 550-2611
- Alliance Francaise, 1345 Bush Street, (415) 775-7755
- Peek-a-Boutique, 1306 Castro Street, (415) 641-6192

Newspapers
- *San Francisco Chronicle*, (415) 777-7777
- *Marina Times*, (415) 928-1398
- *Potrero View*, (415) 824-7516
- *Noe Valley Voice*, (415) 821-3324
- *El Mensajero*, (Spanish language) (415) 206-7235

College and University Postings
- University of San Francisco (USF) Student Career Services: To receive by fax a "babysitter list" free of charge, call (415) 422-6216.
- City College of San Francisco (CCSF) Student Career Services: Job announcements are sent to the Child Development Department and all nine campuses. See www.ccsf.org/career/employer. Announcements can also be faxed to (415) 550-4400. For more information call (415) 550-4346.
- San Francisco State University (SFSU) Student Career Services: No charge. Job listings are posted in job binders for one week. About 30 students review the listings daily. Send by mail to Career Center, San Francisco State University, San Francisco, CA 94132-4042, or fax to *(415) 338-2979*. Alternatively, post online for a $17 fee at www.sfsu.edu.

Child Care Resource and Referral Networks
Children's Council of San Francisco
575 Sutter Street, 2nd Floor
San Francisco, CA 94102
(415) 243-0111 Referral
Children@childrenscouncil.org, www.childrenscouncil.org

Wu Yee Children's Services
888 Clay Street, Lower Level
San Francisco, CA 94108
(415) 391-4956 Referral

MARIN COUNTY

Bulletin Boards
- Center for Creative Parenting, 2217 Larkspur Landing, Larkspur, (415) 461-8323
- Jewish Community Center, 200 North San Pedro Road, San Rafael, (415) 430-2432, (415) 479-2000
- Parents Place Marin, 440 Civic Center Drive, San Rafael, (415) 491-7959
- Parents Place, 680 Wilson Ave., Novato, (415) 491-7959
- Canal Community Alliance, 91 Larkspur Street, San Rafael, (415) 454-2640, *fax (415) 454-3967*

Newspapers:
- *Marin Independent Journal*, (415) 883-8666
- *Marin Scope (Marin Scope, Mill Valley Herald, Twin City Times, Ross Valley Reporter, News Pointer)*, (415) 289-4040 x25

College and High School Bulletin Boards and Web Sites
- Dominican College, San Rafael, Student Development Office: *fax (415) 257-1399*
- College of Marin, Career Center: *fax (415) 457-3896*
- College of Marin, Early Childhood Education Dept: Call Sandy Kallenberg at (415) 485-9369
- Tamalpais High School, Mill Valley, Student Career Services: *fax (415) 380-3506*
- Redwood High School, Larkspur, Student Career Services: (415) 924-3616

Child Care Resource and Referral Networks
Marin Child Care Council
555 Northgate Drive
San Rafael, CA 94903
(415) 479-CARE Referral
stephanie@mc3.org, www.mc3.org

EAST BAY
Bulletin Boards
* Banana's, 5232 Claremont Avenue, Oakland, (510) 658-7101

Newspapers
* *Oakland Tribune*, (800) 595-9595
* *Contra Costa Newspapers (Montclarion, Piedmonter, Berkeley Voice, Contra Costa Times, San Ramon Valley Times, West Coast Times, Oakland Hills El Cerrito Journal, Alameda Journal)*, (510) 339-8777
* U.C. Berkeley *Daily Californian*, (510) 548-8300

University and College Bulletin Boards and Web Sites
* www.parents.berkeley.edu. This U.C. Berkeley Parent's Network site contains thousands of recommendations and great advice from the UCB Parents mailing list, a volunteer-run e-mail newsletter for parents affiliated with University of California, Berkeley.
* U.C. Berkeley Student Employment Office: (510) 642-0440 (call for information on how to post a notice)
* Las Madonnas Community College: (925) 439-2181
* Mills College Children's School, Oakland: *fax (510) 430-3379*
* Mills College Student Career, Oakland: *fax (510) 430-3235*
* Diablo Valley College, Pleasant Hill, Job Placement Office: Call (925) 685-1230 x206 for form to fax to *(925) 691-7538*
* Contra Costa Community College, Student Development Office: *fax (510) 231-0327*

Child Care Resource and Referral Networks
4Cs of Alameda County
22351 City Center Drive, Suite 200
Hayward, CA 94541
(510) 582-2182 Referral - Hayward Area
(510) 790-0655 Referral - Tri-Cities Area

Banana's
5232 Claremont Avenue
Oakland, CA 94618
(510) 658-0381
Bananainc@aol.com

Child Care Links
1020 Serpentine Lane, Suite 102
Pleasanton, CA 94566
(925) 417-8733 Referral/Administration
(925) 417-8740 fax
RFD1@ix.netcom.com

Contra Costa Child Care Council
1035 Detroit Avenue, Suite 200
Concord, CA 94518
(925) 676-5442 Administration

Contra Costa Child Care Council
2280 Diamond Blvd., Suite 500
Concord, CA 94520
(925) 676-5437 Referral - Central Contra Costa County

Contra Costa Child Care Council
3104 Delta Fair Blvd.
Antioch, CA 94806
(925) 778-4739 Referral - Eastern Contra Costa County

Contra Costa Child Care Council
3065 Richmond Parkway, Suite 112
Richmond, CA 94806
(510) 233-KIDS Referral - Western Contra Costa County

PENINSULA/SOUTH BAY
Bulletin Boards
- Peninsula Parents Place, 410 Sherman Ave., Palo Alto, (650) 688-3040
- Jewish Family and Children's Services, Belmont, (650) 591-8991

Newspapers
- *San Jose Mercury News*, (408) 920-5111
- *Los Altos Town Crier*: Los Altos, Los Altos Hills and Mountain View, (650) 948-9000
- *San Jose Metro*: Los Gatos, Saratoga, Cupertino, Willow Glen, and Sunnyvale, (408) 298-8000
- *Palo Alto Weekly*, *Mountain View Voice*, and *The Almanac* (*The Almanac* serves Menlo Park, Portola Valley, Atherton, Woodside), (650) 326-8210, or www.paloaltoonline.com
- *Palo Alto Daily News*: Sunnyvale/Mt. View to Millbrae & Burlingame, (650) 327-6397 x 301
- *San Mateo Times*, (650) 348-4459
- *El Observador* (bilingual Spanish/English), (408) 543-2944

Universities and Colleges
- Canada Community College, Redwood City, Student Career Center: Fax announcement to be placed in binders to *(650) 306-3457*, or post job on Jobtrak (1-800-999-8725 www.jobtrack.com) for a small fee. For more information call the Student Counseling/Career Services at (650) 306-3452
- Diablo Valley Community College, Student Career Services, *fax (925) 691-7538*
- De Anza Community College, Cupertino, Student Career Center, *fax (408) 864-5627*, or www.deanza.fhda.edu/career
- Foothill Community College, Los Altos, *fax (650) 949-7375*
- San Jose City College, San Jose, Job Placement Office: To post a position call (408) 288-3794 for instructions, or fax information to *(408) 286-0412* or go to www.sjcc.edu.

Child Care Resource and Referral Networks
Community Coordinated Child Development Council of
Santa Clara County (4Cs)
111 East Gish Road
San Jose, CA 95112
(408) 487-0749 Referral

Child Care Coordinating Council of San Mateo County
700 S. Claremont, Suite 107
San Mateo, CA 94402
(650) 696-8787 Referral

NAPA/SONOMA
Newspapers
- *Napa Valley Register,* (707) 226-3711
- *Vallejo Times Herald,* (707) 255-8456

Universities and Colleges
- Napa Valley Community College, Napa, Student Career Services, *fax (707) 253-3015*
- Sonoma State University, (707) 664-2880
  www.sonoma.edu/university/classifieds

Child Care Resource and Referral Networks
Community Resources for Children
5 Financial Plaza, Suite 224
Napa, CA 94558
(707) 253-0376
(800) 696-4CRC
crc@napanet.net

4Cs of Sonoma County
396 Tesconi Court
Santa Rosa, CA 95401
(707) 522-1410   Referral
www.sonoma4cs.org, info@sonoma4Cs.com

River Child Care Services
P. O. Box 16
Guerneville, CA 95446
rccs@sonic.net
(707) 887-1809   Referral

WEB SITES AND BAY AREA-WIDE RESOURCES

- www.bay-area-sitters.com is a new, free message board for the San Francisco Bay Area to connect parents looking for child care with babysitters and nannies who are looking for jobs.
- www.craigslist.com is a free community-based bulletin board. Look under child care.
- www.nannybank.com
- www.4nannytaxes.com

ADDITIONAL INFORMATION ON DOULAS

Doula training organizations:
Doulas of North America (DONA)
13513 No. Grove Drive
Alpine, Utah 84004
AskDONA@aol.com, www.dona.com
(801) 756-7331 *fax (801) 763-1847*

ALACE (Assn. of Labor Assistants & Childbirth Educators)
P. O. Box 382724
Cambridge, MA 02074
(617) 441-2500, *fax (617) 441-3167*
ALACEHQ@aol.com

Where to find a doula:
• Doulas of North America (see above)
• Organizations dealing with childbirth
• Your birth place (hospital or birth center)
• Your childbirth educator
• Your care provider
• Lactation consultants
• La Leche League members
• Anyone who has recently had a baby or works in the field
• Resources listed below

Bay Area Baby Nurses and Doulas:
Kay Baker, RN
(800) 526-9996 or (415) 899-1889, kbabynurse@aol.com

We Follow the Stork, (510) 802-8282

The First Six Weeks, (510) 232-7678

Birth and Bonding, (510) 527-2121 (Sharon Ledbetter)

Birthways, (510) 548-0845, (510) 869-2797

A Mother's Touch, (415) 456-9166

NANNY ASSOCIATIONS

National Association of Nannies (NAN)
PMB 2004
25 Route 31 South, Suite C
Pennington, NJ 08534
(800) 344-6266

International Nanny Association
Membership Services Office
900 Haddon Avenue, Suite 438
Collingswood, NJ 08108
(856) 858-0808, *fax (856) 858-2519*

California Assn. for the Education of Young Children
P. O. Box 160373
Sacramento, CA 95816-0373
Caeyc@earthlink.net, www.caeyc.org
(916) 486-7750

National Assn. for the Education of Young Children
1509 16th Street, N.W.
Washington, DC 20036-1426
Naeyc@naeyc.org, www.naeyc.org
(800) 424-2460

Nanny News
P. O. Box 190
Princeton, NJ 08542
(800) ME4-NANNY

Bay Area Nanny Association (BANA)
(415) 332-8287
banaemail@aol.com

CPR/FIRST AID TRAINING

Parents should have their nanny attend Red Cross California Child Care Health & Training, which includes Infant and Child CPR (valid for 1 year) and California Child Care First Aid (valid for 3 years) and complies with the California Child care Law for licensing providers.

For San Mateo, San Francisco, Marin County, Contra Costa, Alameda, and Solano counties call (415) 427-8000. For Santa Clara County, call (408) 577-1000; for Napa/Sonoma, call (707) 257-2900. Additional sources for First Aid/CPR training and specific Red Cross locations are listed below.

San Francisco
University of California San Francisco (UCSF)
500 Parnassus Avenue, Level H, Room 006, (415) 476-1817
Monthly 8:30 a.m.-4:30 p.m.

Perinatal Education and Lactation Center
3698 California Street, (415) 346-BABY

Natural Resources
1307 Castro Street, (415) 550-2611

Marin County
American Red Cross
712 Fifth Avenue, San Rafael, (415) 721-2365

Center for Creative Parenting
Larkspur Landing, (415) 461-8323
Monthly evening classes

East Bay
Banana's
5232 Claremont Avenue, Oakland, (510) 658-7101

American Red Cross
373 North L Street, Livermore, (925) 294-7800

Peninsula /South Bay
American Red Cross
1710 Truesdale Avenue, Burlingame, (650) 259-1757

Child Care Coordinating Council (4C's)
700 S. Claremont, Suite 107, San Mateo, (650) 696-8787
Monthly classes

PUBLIC HEALTH CLINICS

San Francisco County
Sunset District
1351 24th Avenue (at Irving), (415) 753-8100

Adult Immunization Clinic (TB, Hepatitis A & B)
101 Grove St., #405, (415) 554-2625

Castro/Mission District
3850 17th Street, (415) 487-7500

Chinatown District
1490 Mason Street, (415) 705-8500

Outer Mission District
1525 Silver Avenue, (415) 715-0300

Western Addition
1302 Pierce (corner of Ellis), (415) 292-1300

Marin County
Marin County Department of Health and Human Services
910 D Street (at 3rd)

San Rafael, (415) 499-7084
TB testing is done on Tuesdays from 12-4 p.m. and is free.
Hep A/B immunizations require 2-3 visits and cost $130-$150 per visit.

Napa County
Napa County Department of Health and Human Services
2344 Old Sonoma Road, Napa
(707) 253-4807

Sonoma County
Sonoma County Department of Health and Human Services
3420 Chanat Road, Sonoma
(707) 565-4820

East Bay
Concord (925) 646-5275
Pittsburgh (925) 427-8034
Richmond (510) 374-3101
Berkeley, 830 University Avenue, (510) 665-7300

Santa Clara County
For TB testing, (408) 792-5200 or www.scctravelclinic.org

Public walk-in clinics:
• 660 Fair Oaks Ave. (near El Camino), Sunnyvale
  Monday, 8:30 a.m. - 11 a.m., 1 p.m. - 4 p.m.
• Park Alameda Clinic, 976 Lenzen Ave./The Alameda
  San Jose, M, Tu, Wed, Fri, 8:30 a.m. - 4 p.m.
• East San Jose, 1993 McKee Rd (near Jackson)
  M, Tu, Wed, Fri, 8:30 a.m. - 11 a.m., 1 p.m. - 4 p.m.

SUPPORT SPECIFICALLY FOR LESBIAN & GAY PARENTS

Our Family, the Bay Area Gay & Lesbian Family Group, was formed in 1994, and now includes more than 300 families throughout the Bay Area. Our Family publishes a quarterly newsletter, has a web site and offers a weekly e-mail update. It also provides workshops on gay and lesbian parenting issues. The Grandparents, Aunts and Uncles Program matches singles and couples without children with families. Our Family, P. O. Box 13505, Berkeley, CA 94712-4505, (510) 540-7774, www.ourfamily.org.

TRANSLATION & INTERPRETATION SERVICES

• Inlingua, (888) 558-3775, inlingua@ix.netcom.com

• All Language Alliance, (303) 470-9555,
  www.languagealliance.com

GROUP INSURANCE

Kaiser-Permanente, Personal Advantage Policy
www.kp.org/california, (800) 464-4000

Blue Cross Blue Shield, Individual Plans,
(800) 450-8001, www.calhealth.net

www.healthcareshopper.com, (800) 557-5693

Melita-McDonald Insurance Agency
(408) 882-0800, x134

Child Care Staffing
5146 Amelia Earhart Drive
Salt Lake City, Utah 84116
(800) 648-3949

Richard Eisenberg Associates
Newton Centre, MA
(800) 777-5675

NANNYCAMS

- Citikids, 152 Clement St., San Francisco, (415) 752-3837
- www.eaprotection.com
- www.knowyournanny.com, (800) 454-2062

PARENTING AGENCIES
& MOTHERS' GROUPS

For a detailed listing of mothers' groups throughout
the Bay Area, see www.geocities.com:0080/sfbamc and
www.parentspress.com.

San Francisco
Parents Place
3272 California Street
(415) 563-1041

Natural Resources
1307 Castro Street
(415) 550-2611

Perinatal Education and Lactation Center
3698 California Street
(415) 346-BABY

Golden Gate Mothers Group
(500+ members in SF, mothers "pregnant to preschool")
(415) 789-7219, www.ggmg.org

Marin County
Center for Creative Parenting
2217 Larkspur Landing, Larkspur
(415) 461-8323

Parents Place Marin
440 Civic Center Drive, San Rafael
(415) 491-7959

Jewish Community Center
200 North San Pedro Road, San Rafael, (415) 430-2432,
    (415) 479-2000

San Rafael Mothers' Club, www.srmoms.org

East Bay
Banana's
5232 Claremont Avenue, Oakland, (510) 658-7101

East Bay MOMS
www.eastbaycomo.com

Peninsula/South Bay
Peninsula Parents Place, 410 Sherman Ave., Palo Alto
(650) 688-3032

Jewish Family and Children's Services, Belmont
(650) 591-8991

The Mothers' Club of Palo Alto/Menlo Park
www.batnet.com/momsclub

San Jose MOMS, www.bayareamoms.org

Burlingame Mothers' Club, www.burlingamemothers.org

San Mateo Mothers' Club, (650) 286-3404

Napa/Sonoma County
Petaluma Mothers Club, (707) 778-6494

Santa Rosa Mothers Club
www.pressdemocrat.com/community/mothersclub

Sonoma Valley Mothers' Club (Sonoma to Kenwood)
(707) 252-5202

Mothers of Multiples
• Contra Costa Parents of Multiples, (925) 431-8355
• Marin Mothers of Multiples, (415) 460-9049
• San Francisco Mothers of Twins Club, (415) 440-TWINS
• Tri-Cities Mothers of Multiples, (510) 888-4444
• Twins by the Bay (twins & triplets), (510) 655-4139
• Santa Clara County Mothers of Multiples
  (408) 535-0391
• Mid-Peninsula Mothers of Twins Club, (650) 599-2022
• National Organization of Mothers of Twins Club
  (877) 540-2200, www.nomotc.org

SICK CHILD CARE & EMERGENCY BACK-UP

Be sure to line up emergency and back-up care before you need it. (You may have to visit a center and register your child before using its services.) Child Care Resource and Referral agencies in all counties can direct you to a family day care or child care center when you need temporary, last-minute back-up care or care for a mildly-ill child. In addition, most nanny placement agencies handle temporary child care.

Whim Agency
(415) 383-9446, www.whimagency.com
Provides on-call assistance in San Francisco, So. San Francisco, Marin County, and the East Bay.

Well-Center
Fairfax/San Anselmo Children's Center, San Anselmo
(415) 454-1811. A community-based service for families. They will care for mildly-ill children ages 3 mos.–10 years. A site visit and completion of paperwork is required prior to using the center.

BAY AREA NANNY PLACEMENT AGENCIES

Most nanny agencies place nannies in counties other than the one in which their office is located. Most agencies place permanent and temporary nannies who work either full-time or part-time. Not all agencies are created equal. Refer to page 99 for questions to ask agencies to determine whether they will be a good match for you.

San Francisco and Marin County
Aunt Ann's Home Care (San Francisco)
Contact: Denise Collins, (415) 974-3530
Established in 1958. Family-owned business for three generations. No registration fee. Permanent and temporary child care, as well as baby nurses.

Town & Country Resources (Larkspur)
Contact: Cindy Lee-Gong, (415) 461-7755
Established in 1982. The largest agency with offices in San Francisco, Larkspur, Palo Alto, and Campbell. Registration fee of $250. Permanent and temporary child care, emergency and sick child care.

Rent a Parent Personnel Services (Tiburon)
Contact: Dianna Chiarabano, (415) 435-2642
Established in 1984. No registration fee. Permanent and temporary, emergency child care.

Kidz Biz Nanny Search (Pacifica)
Contact: Shelley McKeever, (650) 738-0848

Napa/Sonoma
Nannies of the Valley Placement Agency (Napa)
Contact: Sarah Lane, (707) 251-8035

The Mom Connection Referral Agency (Auburn)
Contact: Maxine Dunsmore, (530) 886-8817
Considerable experience in nanny placement field. No registration fee. Permanent, temporary, part-time and full-time child care.

East Bay
A Nanny Connection (Danville)
Contact: Robin, (925) 957-0358

Be In Our Care Agency, Inc. (Walnut Creek)
Contact: Bea Littlejohn, (925) 933-2273
Established in 1985. No registration fee. Permanent, temporary, part-time and full-time child care.

Nannies 4 Families, Inc. (Hercules)
Contact: Kimberly Johnson, (510) 222-9747
The owner has eight years' experience in nanny field. No registration fee. Permanent, temporary, part-time and full-time child care.

The Nanny Network, Inc. (Walnut Creek)
Contact: Susan Stimmel, (925) 256-8575
The owner began this business after her experience hiring a nanny in 1992. No registration fee. Permanent, temporary, full-time and part-time child care.

Peninsula and South Bay
Bay Area 2nd Mom, Inc. (Palo Alto)
Contact: Shalini Azariah, (650) 858-2469

California Nanny Network, LLC (San Jose)
Contact: Kate Grabenkort, (408) 260-9125

Stanford Park Nannies (Menlo Park & Los Gatos)
Contact: Daryl Camarillo, Maggie Doyle, (650) 462-4580
Agency owners have more than 17 years of combined nanny referral experience. $150 registration fee. Permanent nannies who make a one-year commitment.

EF AuPair, Cambridge, MA
(617) 619-1100
Established in 1989. $250 registration fee. Au-pairs make a one-year commitment to provide child care in exchange for room/board and the experience of living in the U.S.

NOTES

Finding a Preschool for Your Child in San Francisco
$19.95
By Lori Rifkin, Ph.D., Vera Obermeyer, Ph.D., and Irene Byrne
ISBN 0-9648757-2-1
Expert advice on choosing from more than 150 private and public preschools in San Francisco. Profiles of preschools.

Private Schools of San Francisco & Marin Counties (K-8)
$19.95
By Susan Vogel
ISBN 1-930074-02-6
More than 80 private elementary schools in San Francisco and Marin. Extensive discussion of admission process. 4th edition.

Private High Schools of the San Francisco Bay Area (2nd Ed)
$21.95
By Susan Vogel
ISBN: 0-9648757-9-9
More than 50 private high schools in the Bay Area from Marin through San Jose plus East Bay (8 counties). Updates and map.

High School Admission Workbook
$14.95
By Susan Vogel
Available only from Pince-Nez Press (not in bookstores). This 50-page spiral bound workbook helps parents and kids prepare for and organize the grueling high school admission process.

Private Schools of the San Francisco Peninsula/Silicon Valley
$19.95
By Ellen S. Lussier
ISBN: 0-9648757-6-4
Private elementary and middle schools from Burlingame through San Jose (San Mateo and Santa Clara counties). 188 pages.

For other and upcoming books, see www.pince-nez.com

ORDER FORM

Please send me ___ copy(ies) of *Finding a Nanny for Your Child in the San Francisco Bay Area*

at $19.95 per copy $_____

ADD price of any book on the previous page $_____

SUBTOTAL $_____

ADD applicable sales tax (8.25% in SF) $_____

ADD shipping/handling: for the first book,
$2.50 for book rate or $4.00 for priority rate $_____

for each additional book, add $.75 for book rate
or $1.00 for priority $_____

If you want the book sent to an address other than the one on your check, please provide it:

Name:_____

Address: _____

City: _____State ____ Zip: _____

Mail this form and your check **made out to Pince-Nez Press** to:

Pince-Nez Press/Order
1459 18th St., PMB 175
San Francisco, CA 94107

Or order by credit card at www.pince-nez.com